LIMON, COLORADO

HUB CITY OF THE HIGH PLAINS
1888 - 1952

BY JAMES E. FELL, JR.

LIMON
HERITAGE
SOCIETY

This project was partially funded by a State Historical Fund grant from the Colorado Historical Society, with additional funding from friends of the Limon Heritage Museum. The project also included an exhibit, Limon's Invincible Spirit: Early Limon to 1952; *a Heritage Walking Tour; and a Children's Study Guide.*

On the cover: A typical summer afternoon in Limon in 1941 — the Colorado Springs section of the Rocky Mountain Rocket with an AB6 unit waits to combine with the Denver E6630.

(From an original acrylic painting by Mike Danneman.)

Printed in the United States of America
Johnson Publishing, Boulder, CO 80301
Lucille Reimer, Typesetting
Vivian Lowe, Graphic Design

Library of Congress Cataloging-in-Publication Data 97-72248
ISBN: 0-9658428-0-0

Table of Contents

The Land Office of William S. Pershing, Limon's principal founder, ca. 1900. *Pikes Peak Library Collection*

Photographer Erv Malcom captured this 1908 summer outing to the Limon depot.

ACKNOWLEDGMENTS

Many individuals have contributed to the development of this book, and I would like to recognize their assistance here, although there are too many to name all individually. Thanks go to many people living in Limon and other communities who graciously took time from their schedules to fill out questionnaires, speak with the author, and critique the manuscript. The Limon town government and staff provided the minutes of the Town Board and also offered a comfortable research space in the Town Board chamber. JC's Deli offered a pleasant venue for many conversations and interviews. Personnel at the Limon Memorial Library also provided time and space during the research phase of the book; so, too, have the staffs of other libraries in Denver and Colorado Springs. The Colorado Historical Society in particular, through State Historical Fund grants, provided assistance for both the research and publication of the book.

I would like to recognize the contribution of a number of new friends. Special thanks go to Chuck Stone and Helen Christenson, who provided substantial information about Limon's development and who devoted many hours to reviewing the manuscript; to Irma Kjosness, Mable Burgess, Grace Swanson, Betty Slater, Nadine Garnhart, Jim Statton, Dawn Walker, Norma Grenawalt, Bob Coulson, Terry Blevins, and numerous members of the Limon Heritage Society and Limon's Hub City Seniors who shared their insights; to Lucille Reimer, who set the type; and to Vivian Lowe and Harold Lowe, who sponsored the project, guided its development, and ultimately brought *Limon* into print.

Preface

Driving west across the plains on I-70 brings you into ever more arid country. From the lush, rolling hills of Missouri, the road leads west across the parched Kansas plains into eastern Colorado, then up, up, up, till it reaches the point of a high, almost imperceptible escarpment that looks like an arrowhead pushing its way from the mountains into the high plains. At the back wings of the arrowhead lie Denver to the north and Colorado Springs to the south. At the point of the arrowhead lies the town of Limon, Colorado.

Limon owes its origin and development to its role as a transportation and distribution center. Historically, there was water here — water provided by the Big Sandy, a small stream that meanders easterly across the high plains. That was enough to bring the Smoky Hill Trail through the area. Pioneers could find water for themselves and their livestock on the thirsty route across the plains to Denver. Later, the Kansas Pacific Railroad followed the same general route as it put down rails to the Mile High City.

But neither the Smoky Hill Trail nor the Kansas Pacific Railroad produced a settlement. That would have to wait until the late 1880s when the Rock Island Railroad crossed the old Kansas Pacific, now the Union Pacific, track at a place almost inadvertently named Limon's Camp. As the town grew up at this crossing, it became a center for raising cattle and sheep herding, a division point for the Rock Island Railroad, and a locus of what was called dryland farming.

Though spare and unpretentious, early-day Limon attracted determined pioneers from many parts of the United States and Europe. Some moved into town. Others chose to live in even smaller settlements like Walk's Camp and Pleasant Plains that dotted the prairie. Still others put up sod houses on isolated homesteads where they struggled to wrest a living from the earth. Wherever they chose to settle, all of these people lived in a sunbaked land characterized by brown undulating hills, distant vistas, deep blue skies, steady northern winds, scant water, and windmills built to draw water from the earth. By the early 20th century, they had made Limon the hub city of the high plains.

This is Limon's story — from its founding in the late 1880s to its heyday in the 1940s and early 1950s.

* * * * *

Limon, Colorado, 1908. "Land of Sunshine, Wealth, and Windmills."

This book is dedicated to
Charles W. Stone, Helen S. Christenson,
and Lincoln County Historian Mary Liz Owen.

Laying railroad track near Limon's Camp, 1888.

By tradition, Limon, Colorado, takes its name from John Limon, a construction foreman on the Chicago, Rock Island, and Pacific Railroad. But of John Limon, nothing is known — nothing of his origins, nothing of his career, and nothing of his ultimate destiny. Nothing except that he established a camp here so that the Rock Island line could lay track to connect the high plains to Denver and Colorado Springs. Who John Limon was may never be known, but his work at this site in the late 1880s, the place where the Rock Island line crossed the Union Pacific track, encapsulated the future of the town that bears his name. Limon, Colorado, would owe its origin and development, its hard times and prosperity, largely to its role as a transportation and distribution center on the high plains of Eastern Colorado.

Origins

In the course of the 1880s — in the heyday of western railway construction — the Chicago, Rock Island, and Pacific Railroad made plans to lay track across the Kansas and Colorado plains to the Rocky Mountains beyond. The Rock Island intended to have a single track cross the plains into Eastern Colorado. Then it would branch as it approached the mountains — one track going to Denver, the principal rail center in Colorado; the other track heading to Colorado Springs, where it would link up with the Colorado Midland Railroad, the first standard gauge line through the Rocky Mountains.

With its plans formulated, the Rock Island pushed ahead, and in the late 1880s, it began to put down rails in Eastern Colorado. A key question the road had to answer was where to establish the division point for trains going to Denver and Colorado Springs. Given that the Union Pacific Railroad had already established a division point at Hugo, the Rock Island chose a site some ten miles west, on the Union Pacific track. This is where John Limon (possibly Lyman or Lymon) established his camp.

Construction began in two directions in March 1888. From Limon's Camp,

View of South Limon and surrounding country. *T.A. Pershing Collection*

railroad workers built west toward Colorado Springs and east toward Goodland, Kansas (another division point). The Rock Island shipped in all kinds of equipment, some coming overland and some on the Union Pacific's rails. (1)

As the railroad took shape, Limon's Camp quickly became a well-known destination point. It probably emerged first as a cluster of tents and a jumble of ties, rails, and a host of other construction materials. But that was temporary. The Rock Island soon built a small roundhouse, a coal chute, a section house, and an eating house to serve its trains and passengers. Even so, living conditions were spartan for the first residents. Most workmen, and their families, lived in boxcars and tiny houses just north of the roundhouse. There, a few business places sprang to life on the dusty street. And Limon's Camp gradually evolved into the small spare town of Limon Station. (2)

Railroads and Livestock

The livestock industry was the first to benefit directly from the Rock Island's arrival. Cattle-raising here was nothing new — it stretched back to the 1860s when ranchers began grazing cattle on the open range on both sides of the Big Sandy, the small stream that flowed in a broad arc across the plains to the Arkansas River. The earliest cattlemen had driven their herds to Denver and the mining camps farther west. Later ranchers added Colorado Springs as a market. The cattlemen did not have the high plains to themselves, however. The first sheep ranchers arrived in the 1870s. Some pioneers — like Russell Gates — raised both sheep and cattle, although the cattlemen got most of the publicity.

Cattlemen had their individual brand or brands. Fred Jenny, who grazed his cattle on the range south of the Big Sandy, branded INN on the left side of his cattle. Alex Urquhart, whose range was on Middlemist Creek, used the ΛUΛ . S. McCully was fancier. He used an (8) for the cattle he grazed on the range near Walk's Camp. Thompson and Bonary, who grazed their cattle on the range south of the Big Sandy, used a simple PT — for Porter Thompson himself, the principal owner.

These cattle ranchers had several things in common. They grazed their herds in and about Limon and listed their address as Limon Station. They probably belonged to the Lincoln County Cattle Growers' Association, which generally met at Hugo, the county seat. And they had their champion in the Hugo *Range Ledger*, "dedicated to the live stock interests of Eastern Colorado."

The most important of these cattle ranchers was Porter Thompson. He came to Colorado from St. Joseph, Missouri, in the early 1890s, and with various partners, ran cattle on the open range as far east as Kansas. Thompson had considerable foresight. He was among the first to realize that the days of the open range near Limon were numbered. As a result, he and his partners were among the first near Limon to carve out individual ranches and to begin fencing the range with barbed wire. Like Russell Gates, Porter would have an important impact on Limon's development. (3)

But if cattle got most of the publicity, Lincoln County also had its share of sheep growers. They raised sheep primarily for wool, not lamb or mutton. They, too, met in Hugo as the Lincoln and Elbert Counties Wool Growers Association. (4)

Time out for a picnic on the Porter Thompson Ranch, 1908.

Early-Day Limon

Although Limon had evolved in the late 1880s, the *State Business Directory* did not take notice until 1893. That year, it finally listed the community as "Limon Station." The editors noted simply that it was an "Agricultural Town in Lincoln County, on the U.P. & C.R.I.R'y. Population 100." Of its residents, Miss M. Alley worked as a "teacher." J.W. Connolly ran the "RR boarding house," whereas S. McCully, the sometime rancher, had only a "boarding house." C.H. Sandstead had a "hotel & saloon" while Freel Brothers dealt in general merchandise and G.D. Freel served as postmaster. (5)

Despite the devastating depression that convulsed the nation after the Panic of 1893, Limon grew steadily. In 1894, the *State Business Directory* noted that "grazing and stock raising [was the] principal industry." Miss Alley the teacher was no longer listed, but besides Connolly, Freel Brothers, McCully, and Sanstad (the spelling corrected from the previous year), there was a new listing — that of J.J. Grier, who ran the "R.R. eating house."

But businesses came and went. In the mid-1890s, James Fitzgibbons took over Sanstad's saloon, only to be succeeded by R. Beistline, who in turn became Limon's postmaster. J.F. Kuhn arrived to become the town's first physician. The *Limon Independent*, published by E.P. Montgomery, sprang to life as the first newspaper. Also coming to town were two other enterprises destined for a long stay when F. Tompkins opened his "saloon," which by 1900 he had expanded into a "saloon & hotel," and when the cattle and sheep rancher Russell Gates opened a branch of his Russell Gates Company, which dealt in "genl mdse". (6)

The Tompkins Hotel, the Russell Gates Mercantile Company, and Tom Bell's Pool Hall were to become Limon business fixtures.

As the 20th century dawned, Limon's population, once as high as 125 people, suddenly dropped to 75 persons, but still more new faces appeared on the business scene. One was Thomas J. Bell, or simply Tom Bell, first listed as the proprietor of a "barber & pool room." In the years to come, his hotel and rooming house would join the Russell Gates Mercantile Company, Grier's railway eating house, and Tompkins saloon & hotel as fixtures in Limon's business establishments focusing on railroad traffic.

When the population surged to 150 in 1904, the *Business Directory* listed the town simply as "Limon" for the first time. By now, there were many new businesses. Besides such standbys as Bell, Russell Gates, Grier, and Tompkins, Limon had A. Bardsdale as its auctioneer, Thomas Cope working a blacksmith shop, Pershing & Meehan in real estate, and an office of the Western Union Telegraph Company. F.M. Carman had his "books & stationery, cigars, confecty, drugs, jeweler, notary public and postmaster." Hans Christenson, an enterprising immigrant from Norway, appeared the next year, and soon described himself as the purveyor of "wines, liquors and cigars." And the community saw the arrival of its first bank — the Limon State Bank — James McClure cashier.

As Limon's hinterlands grew with the rise of farming, real estate agents multiplied in town. Among them was C.M. Immel, who was both the Union Pacific agent in town and the vice president of the Campbell System Farming

Association, which had pioneered important dryland farming techniques, such as the shallow planting of seed. He advertised himself and his firm, C.M. Immel & Company, as "Land and Immigration Agents," which meant that they had "an established business" and owned "several large tracts of land" which they would "sell on from 5 to 10 years time." Furthermore, Immel and Company had "some good homesteads...yet open adjoining our lands upon which we locate persons purchasing. Good crops grown in this district under Campbell System Farming."

The Annex, seen here under construction, was a popular early day rooming house. It was moved in 1940 and was still in use in the late 1990s.

Not to be outdone by Immel was William S. Pershing. He listed himself as the "special sales agent for Union Pacific lands" and noted that he was "county surveyor for Lincoln County." He also styled himself as giving a "boost for the land of sunshine and wealth, where the Campbell System wins." By the end of the decade, however, when Immel virtually disappeared, Pershing styled himself as "the pioneer land man of Eastern Colorado," a man who had "valuable information for homeseekers and investors. Free maps, folders, etc. furnished on application." Pershing was doing well, but his Limon career was only beginning.

Joining Immel and Pershing was the W.E. Epperson Land & Investment Company. It also took out a huge advertisement in the *State Business Directory* where it listed itself as in Limon, although it operated out of the Opera House Block in Denver. Epperson's firm proclaimed that it had "improved and unimproved farms." All of them were "close to town and market — nothing better to be found anywhere — be sure to look this over before you buy elsewhere — best of soil, best of water, good neighbors, good schools. We sell our own lands," and, of course, the lands were in the "rain belt of Colorado."

These advertisements clearly reflected a shift in the economy — dryland farming had come to the high plains. The farmers came from everywhere — Kansas and Texas, Minnesota and Washington, to name several states. Others arrived from Europe. Michael A. Milano, had come to the United States from

Lake, Colorado, no longer exists, but in 1903 it was a tiny, Union Pacific stop with a small depot, water tower, pump house, sod house, loading chute, and section house.

Lux Collection

Campo Boss, Italy, in 1878, at the age of 15; he and his wife took up a homestead in 1910. Most of the new farmers, however, were of Scandinavian heritage — immigrants themselves or the sons and daughters of immigrants. (7)

A.C. Vallander was a case in point. He was born Axel Kristian Wallander in Sweden in 1869 and emigrated to Concordia, Kansas, in the mid-1880s. He spoke little or no English, and worked there on an uncle's farm. To acculturate, he changed the spelling of his name to Axel Christian Vallender, which preserved the Swedish pronunciation. Then, in 1892, he took a job with the Union Pacific Railroad and gradually made his way west first to Lake, and then to Limon where he worked as a gandy dancer — a railroad worker — on that section of track, eventually becoming section foreman. Quiet and soft-spoken, he never learned to drive, and always traveled by handcar, sometimes with his wife Emma pumping the other end of the walking beam or lever, with their baby Olga lodged in a box on the floor of the handcar. Olga had been born in 1902 in Lake, a tiny railroad water stop, which had once been a stage coach station, burned by the Indians in 1867.

Many people who took up homesteads or bought farmlands arrived in Limon by train on immigrant cars. Glen Raymond Coonts, whose family moved from Kansas, remembered years later that the furniture was in one end of the car and the animals in the other. His experience was typical. (8)

Whatever their expectations, most farmers found that living on the high plains was hard. Many lived in sod houses, even as late as the 1910s. Nate Einertson, for one, termed his home a sod shanty. A Mrs. Drier, who came to Colorado in 1907, lived in a sod barn with the horses. Only later did her family move into what she called "a shack" with a tar paper interior. This was not a whole lot better — particularly after a hailstorm hammered holes in the paper and let the snows pour through the next winter. Esther Johnson, whose family came by immigrant car, lived in "an 8 x 10 shack, no fences, and no well." The

Norwegians were notable homesteaders in the Limon region. Among them were seven families from Selbu, Norway, who settled with others in the Walk's Camp area, where cooperation, tenacity, and stewardship of the land created a legacy for their children and the community.

shack was so small the family had to put its table outdoors at night to provide space to sleep on the floor. And the family had to haul its water two miles, until it could find time to dig a 145-foot well by hand. (9)

The farms had diverse crops — they appear to have been partly commercial and partly self-sustaining. Esther Johnson's family grew so many watermelons that her father put the extras on the road for people to pick up for free. Mrs. Drier's family raised potatoes — which meant that she couldn't go to school until November. During the winter her parents bought flour, rice, and salted herring to get through the cold, hard months. (10)

Fuel was always a problem. There was little wood on the high plains. Some children took large gunny sacks, picked up dried cowchips, and loaded the sacks on lumber wagons. But burning cowchips gave off little heat. To get through the winter, farmers supplemented the cowchips with coal despite the expense. (11)

For children, there were few toys available. Looking back years later, Mrs. Drier remembered that she had no store-bought playthings. Instead, she and the other children made what toys they had out of plants like Russian thistle, which grew in abundance on the dry plains. Some children used broomsticks for make-believe horses. Other made skis out of barrel staves and used them to cross the winter snows to Limon. (12)

Rural children usually went to small, one-room schoolhouses — when they went to school. Both Nate Einertson and Mrs. Drier missed many a class because they had to help their families at harvest time. There was no compulsory attendance, whatever the laws. And the building could be cold, although some farmers tried to furnish wood during the winter months.

School on the plains was far different from school in town. Einertson's teacher taught all eight grades and boarded at students' homes. Glen Coonts' teacher rode a horse to school, and at noon the kids would water their own horses at a draw a half mile away. Mrs. Drier walked three miles to school each day. So, too, did Esther Johnson, who remembered that there were no fences to cross and a lot of half-wild cattle — leftovers, it seems, from the open range days. Sometimes it got dark before she got home, her father would look for her with a lantern, and she would walk toward the light. Later she drove to school in a horse and buggy, but the trail was rough, sometimes little more than a wagon track. (13)

Most students did not remain in school very long. Some went only as far as the eighth grade. (14)

An early parade, possibly celebrating the Fourth of July, makes its way through downtown Limon, ca. 1900. *Pikes Peak Library Collection*

In 1912, Limon opened a high school which became a magnet for those who wanted more education. But to do that, most rural students had to board in town; Limon was too far away to commute. Esther Johnson lived in a dormitory where everyone brought their own food. In later years, Nate and Ida Einertson opened their home to about 30 farm girls attending the high school. (15)

Given the frequently hard times on the plains, Limon provided farmers with the chance for additional income. Michael A. Milano and his wife took up a homestead, but then moved to town where he found work in the Rock Island roundhouse and she found the money to finance various enterprises including the later famous Cozy Cafe. Nate Einertson worked at Limon's bean factory where he sacked and loaded pinto beans. So, too, did Martha Kollath when she moved to Limon in 1939; she picked dirt out of the beans before she got a job sewing shirts at the Tompkins Hotel. (16)

By 1909, Limon's business community was well-established. Immel, Epperson, and Pershing dominated the real estate market both in town and country. J.M. Baily headed the town's only bank — the Limon State Bank. The Russell Gates Mercantile Company, managed by Charles J. Schrader, offered all sorts of "general merchandise" along with "furniture, lumber, coal, grain" and "undertaking." H.A. Mooney's Limon Lumber Company dealt in "lumber and hardware," though it also offered "coal, lime and cement" along with "general building material." And Moorman and Cochran operated the Limon Cement & Brick Company. To take care of travelers, the firm of Christenson & Christenson had its "saloon, restaurant, hotel," along with its "barber shop and pool room in connection." The Grier Hotel Company still ran the Rock Island Eating House.

And Frank Tompkins operated the Hotel Limon with its "first class bar and cafe" and where things were on the "American Plan, $2.00 per day."

There were smaller firms, too. Thomas Cope remained as town blacksmith. Charles J. Schrader served as the local agent for the Caledonian Insurance Company (besides managing the Russell Gates Mercantile). A.W. Miller ran the Limon Drug Company, George W. Pickinpaugh a livery stable, and T.A. Pershing a shoemaking shop. Edward Rusher operated a bakery and O.A. Williams a

Strike up the band! A concert about to begin in front of the Hotel Limon, ca 1900.
Pikes Peak Library Collection

meat market. Limon now had two physicians, L. M. Brady and G.A. Kennedy, the latter destined to have a long career in the community.

Limon got its second newspaper in 1912 when C.T. Rawalt founded the Limon *Express*, which succeeded the *Limon Independent*. Rawalt was a career newspaperman who had founded other papers in eastern Colorado and owned still others in western Colorado, notably at Crested Butte, Gunnison, and Paonia.

Rawalt did not remain long in Limon, however. He sold the paper to J.J. and A.B. Missimer in 1914, then it passed through other hands until Jerry Missimer bought it back in 1922 and renamed it the *Eastern Colorado Leader.* Still later, the paper passed into the hands of Howard Africa, a short, stocky man who became a force in the community until his death in December 1936. Dale and Ronald Cooley purchased the paper in 1937, also acquiring the *Genoa Sentinel* and combining the two papers to form *The Limon Leader.* The Cooley brothers continued a long period of journalistic excellence by the Cooley family in Eastern Colorado. (17)

School buildings came slowly to Limon. The first school opened in a home in the southeast part of town. But finally in 1901, funds were appropriated to build the first schoolhouse located a short distance northwest of the depot. It reportedly had two rooms on one floor, one for the primary grades and one for the upper grades. Ultimately, this structure was converted into apartments when T.J. Bell acquired the building. Limon's first graduating high school class consisted of one individual, Crit Kessinger, son of one of Limon's physicians. (18)

The staff was naturally small. J.H. Albrecht served as principal for a while. Miss E. Kennedy and Miss A. O'Connor taught there at various times, but as with previous principals and teachers, like Ed DeGarmo, "Prof." J.B. Griffith, Miss E. Barrett and Miss M.A. Foote, they stayed in Limon only a year or two. (19)

By 1900, Limon looked like a western town was supposed to look. It was a spare community sprawling out north of the Union Pacific and Rock Island crossing. It had few, if any trees. Its streets were wide and its buildings well-spaced. The business district near the railroad tracks consisted of mostly one and two-story frame structures. Single-story houses dotted the open landscape here and there, but generally north of downtown. Some businesses and some homes had their own windmills because water was scarce.

Mrs. Elmo DeGarmo Rasmus, who lived in Limon during this era, remembered that the town resembled the buildings in the television series *Gunsmoke* (which was popular in the 1960s). Most houses "had a front porch of some kind, and were very old even then," she recalled. "The people who owned cows turned them out in the morning; in the evening we children went in a group and hunted them up."

As on the plains, life for children seemed simple compared to that later. Besides rounding up cows, wrote Mrs. Rasmus, "We hunted wild prairie flowers — One time we girls killed a snake on the way home from school. A man who came along told us it was a rattle snake and asked how you killed it?" One girl said, "Ah, we just pasted him with rocks." Children also rode cowboy ponies when the cowboys were at the "Inn." And they went to Cedar Point on the last day of school where they explored the caves and hunted for petrified wood. She also remembered a sandstorm in the spring. (20)

Limon's religious life developed apace with the town. The Methodist Church originally formed part of a circuit known as the Hugo-Kit Carson Circuit. Riding the circuit was hard. The Reverend E.E. Allison had "the dubious honor" in 1888 when the town began to grow, noted the *Limon Leader.* Women of the church organized the first Sunday School in 1894, but with no money available to build a church, the congregation used the schoolhouse built in 1901 for both a church and Sunday School. When another schoolhouse was built, the church acquired the school. The circuit was finally dissolved in 1909 and Reverend William Johnson named the pastor at $700 a year, plus the parsonage. He also served a mission at Walk's Camp, 16 miles north of Limon. Some preachers traversed the farms surrounding Limon to add members. Most pastors, however, like most school teachers, served only a year or two. (21)

Limon's Baptist Church originated in 1915 when the Railroad Chapel Car arrived under the auspices of the Baptist Home Mission Society. The Church originally had 14 members, but did not obtain a building until 1926. (22)

Outlets for entertainment also grew during these years. At first, there was little to do except to attend school and church social gatherings. One might ride around — "the horse and buggy provided something to do on a sunny afternoon." Townspeople held dances in the municipal hall and parties in private homes. Limon saw its first movie theatre open in 1916; two movies per week, one on Friday and one on Saturday. Basketball games became popular. They took place in the municipal hall — six boys teams and four girls teams — and of course, the high school had both a boys' team and a girls' team. (23)

Summer picnics were popular on the high plains. Pershing's Grove attracted a festively-dressed crowd in 1908.

The town schoolhouse was clearly a community center. Once constructed in 1901, Limonites used it for church, school, court, dances, and public meetings. Functions followed one right after another. One Saturday, the town tried a man for murder. That night, a group held a dance which continued till daylight. On Sunday morning, townspeople held a funeral, and after that, Sunday School. (24)

Limon and the surrounding countryside also endured their share of crime. The most notorious was a double murder committed in 1900. On November 9, Louise Frost, the thirteen-year-old daughter of local ranchers, bought some candy at the Russell Gates store in Limon, then began to drive home in a buggy. She never arrived. As she crossed the Big Sandy near Lake east of town, she was stopped, assaulted, stabbed, and left for dead. When she failed to return home on time, her family began looking, and found her just before she died. Rage gripped the area.

Several days later, Preston Porter, a black teenager working on the railroad near Limon, was apprehended in Denver and charged with the crime. Whether or not he committed the murder is a matter of debate, but Denver police extorted a confession from him to go with circumstantial evidence. With that, Porter was put on a train bound for Hugo "for trial," but his fate was a foregone conclusion. Law enforcement, even Governor Charles S. Thomas, looked the other way. At Lake, a lynch mob took Porter from the train, chained him to a stake on the spot where Louise Frost had died, and burned him alive.

The Town of Limon

Limon grew very rapidly after 1905. The population surged from 150 to 600 people by decade's end, and many social, educational, and religious institutions had developed to complement the steadily growing business community. (25)

Among the people who followed these developments closely was William S. Pershing of Hugo, the land agent for the Union Pacific Railroad. Born in Johnstown, Pennsylvania, in 1852, Pershing had grown up in both Pennsylvania and Illinois (Rock Island, Illinois, by coincidence). After the Civil War, Pershing's family moved to Nebraska, where he went first into farming, and then into buying and selling farms. Pershing seems to have been far more interested in agricultural real estate than in agriculture itself, although the two went hand in hand. He also battled grasshoppers, the scourge of prairie farmers, while he lived in Nebraska. In 1873, just turned twenty-one years old, he married Eliza Jane Beistline, another Pennsylvania native who had moved west with her family to Iowa; they would be married more than 60 years and raise 13 children.

William S. Pershing, Limon's first mayor, key promoter, and major developer.

It was Pershing's interest in land promotion that brought him to Colorado. He moved to Yuma in 1885 and then to Hugo in 1889. He lived there for six years until 1895 when he moved to Limon. He and his partner bought much of the Limon townsite from the Rock Island and Union Pacific Railroad companies, then began subdividing and selling house and business lots. (26)

Pershing the person is hard to pin down. Years later, he would be eulogized as a man of "impeccable character...true and just...a real friend...a gentlemen...always sympathetic, chivalrous, and courteous...a man of high principles and ideals...." Others remembered him as a man who was "tall and slender...reserved...civic-minded." Still others thought he was a scoundrel. Whatever the truth, Pershing now emerged as "the father of Limon." (27)

The construction of the Rock Island line gave Pershing his main chance in life, and he made the most of it. By 1909, his letterhead proclaimed that he was not only county surveyor, but also a man who had "bargains in farms, ranches, and 320-acre homesteads." (28)

That year, Pershing began to spearhead a drive to incorporate Limon. To begin, he and his colleagues developed a town plat. It consisted of four additions. These were Nutting's East and Nutting's West additions; Meehan's Addition, which lay between the two; and Pershing's Addition to the North. On September 12, 1909, the Pershing group properly filed the plat with Lincoln County, in accordance with state law. The county court then appointed Pershing and his colleagues commissioners "for the purpose of holding an election of all the qualified voters of the territory embraced within the limits of said proposed town to vote upon the incorporation of said town."

To incorporate the town, the Pershing group also had to secure the permission of both the Rock Island Railroad and Pershing himself because both owned more than 40 acres of land not surrounded on three sides by platted land. Thus, the organizers had to obtain written permission from both. That was an easy matter. On September 10, T.J. Newkirk, the real estate and tax agent of the Rock Island wrote Pershing that as far as the railroad was concerned, there was "no objection" to enclosing the railroad's property in the town — roughly 57 acres of land and 1.11 miles of track. And naturally, Pershing had no objection as he wrote in his letter "to whom it may concern" on September 20. (29)

By September 20, the five commissioners had secured the names of 38 men and women on a petition to incorporate the town; then they approached the County Court to "pray the appointment" of commissioners to hold an election — and the court appointed Pershing along with Frank Tompkins, Charles J. Schrader, L.M. Brady and Melvin D. Mickle. "At once upon our appointment," they wrote, they "called an election of all qualified electors residing within the territory embraced within the limits of the proposed town of 'LIMON', as described and platted, to be held on the 25th day of October A.D. 1909 at Pershing's office in Limon...." On October 9, they ran the first of the three required notices of election in the Limon *Herald* and posted notices in public places. Then on October 25, acting as the election judges themselves (with two others as clerks), they held the election. Forty-seven men and women voted — 43 for incorporating the town and 4 against. Finally, on November 3, 1909, H.C. Winter, the clerk of the county court, declared the Town of Limon duly incorporated. (30)

Limon encompassed all of Section 17, Township 9 South, Range 56 West, plus small rectangular parts of both Section 19 and Section 20, which lay directly south and west of Section 17. This area would eventually become known as South Limon. It was a strange shape, probably reflecting Pershing's desire to incorporate lands he owned south of the Big Sandy in the new town. But Limon had already developed largely north of the Rock Island/Union Pacific crossing, and that is where Pershing and others platted the townsite, and so Limon took

A bird's eye view of Limon, Colorado, ca. 1910.

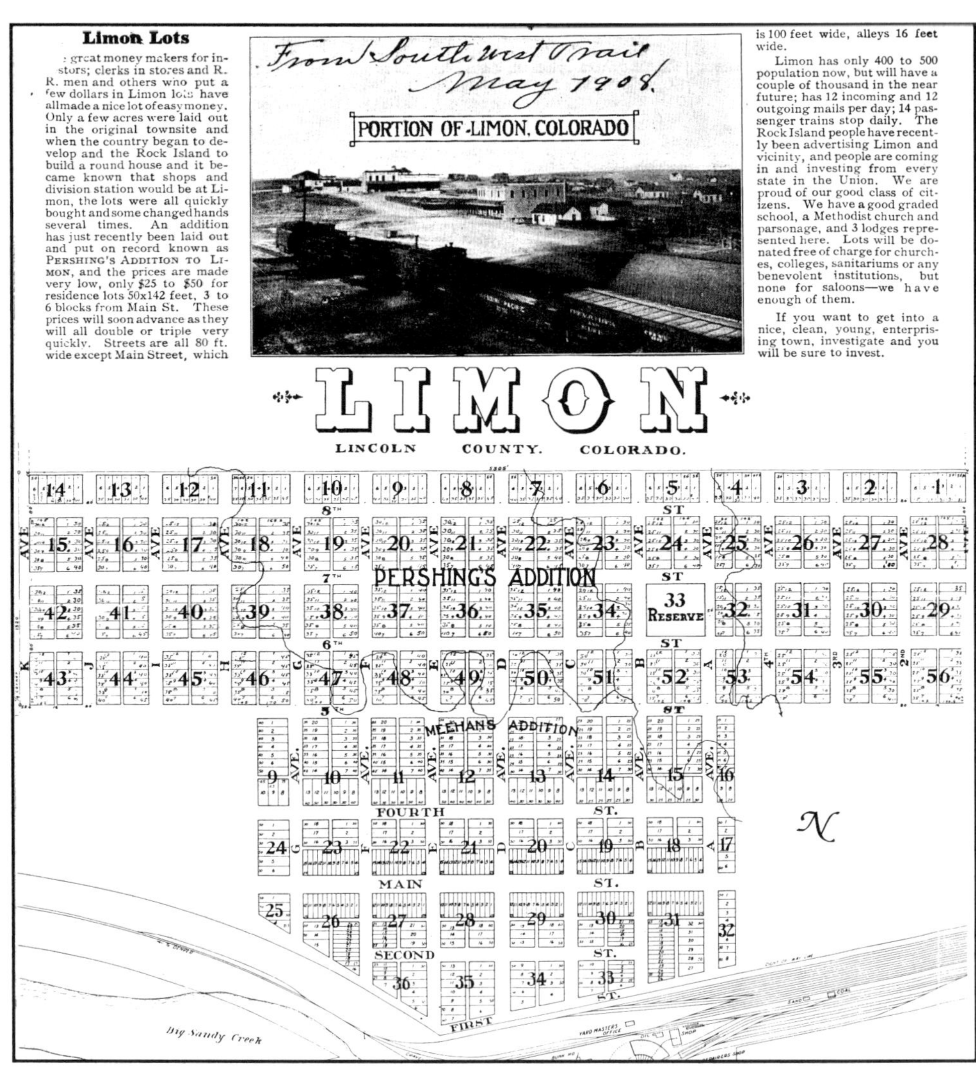

From South West Trail May 1908.

PORTION OF LIMON, COLORADO

Limon Lots

: great money makers for investors; clerks in stores and R. R. men and others who put a few dollars in Limon lots have allmade a nice lot of easy money. Only a few acres were laid out in the original townsite and when the country began to develop and the Rock Island to build a round house and it became known that shops and division station would be at Limon, the lots were all quickly bought and some changed hands several times. An addition has just recently been laid out and put on record known as PERSHING'S ADDITION TO LIMON, and the prices are made very low, only $25 to $50 for residence lots 50x142 feet, 3 to 6 blocks from Main St. These prices will soon advance as they will all double or triple very quickly. Streets are all 80 ft. wide except Main Street, which is 100 feet wide, alleys 16 feet wide.

Limon has only 400 to 500 population now, but will have a couple of thousand in the near future; has 12 incoming and 12 outgoing mails per day; 14 passenger trains stop daily. The Rock Island people have recently been advertising Limon and vicinity, and people are coming in and investing from every state in the Union. We are proud of our good class of citizens. We have a good graded school, a Methodist church and parsonage, and 3 lodges represented here. Lots will be donated free of charge for churches, colleges, sanitariums or any benevolent institutions, but none for saloons—we have enough of them.

If you want to get into a nice, clean, young, enterprising town, investigate and you will be sure to invest.

LIMON

LINCOLN COUNTY. COLORADO.

Limon Town Board Collection

on the appearance of a broad arrowhead pointing south almost directly at the railroad station. South Limon seemed like a peculiar appendage south across the Big Sandy. Yet it was an integral part of the town.

This, then, was the key to Limon's future development. From the Rock Island/Union Pacific crossing, the east-west streets ran from First to Eighth, although what would have been Third Street was named Main Street. The thoroughfares running north-south were the avenues, beginning with 1st, 2nd, and 3rd on the east side of town, then changing to letters A through K as they moved to the west, a total of 14 blocks. This design put the railroad station on First Street and E Avenue. That would be the heart of downtown during the railroad era that lasted to midcentury. South of First Street lay the railroad tracks, the wye, the turntable, and roundhouse. Still farther south flowed the Big Sandy.

Town Development

With Limon duly incorporated, the trustees created the town's government at meetings generally held every other week in Pershing's office, the unofficial town hall — a practice that continued for years. Pershing became the first mayor, and the first board of trustees reflected the business community — the group that would provide Limon's leadership throughout the century. The first board passed ordinances to regulate life in town and appointed the first public officials.

Much of this work took place early in 1910. The first town treasurer, F.M. Carman, earned a salary of $1.00 per month, although he had to post a $2,000 bond. The first city marshal, J.H. Lindamoode, received a salary of $20 per month "in addition to such fees as provided by ordinance." The board passed ordinances on licenses, dogs, animals, public carriers, and real estate brokers (though the last was quickly repealed). Later in the year, the board granted certain privileges to the Colorado Telephone Company, which put up a $10,000 bond in 1911. (31)

Pershing and his colleagues also took up the crucial question of water — specifically building waterworks to resolve Limon's chronic shortage. In July 1910, they agreed to hold a special election that would authorize the trustees "to erect water works for fire and domestic purposes to be owned, managed and operated by the town." The vote was held in Pershing's office on August 9, and the populace approved by a count of 42 to 7. Later, the trustees voted unanimously to pay Pershing $125 for "a sight" for the "tower and tank." By October, the project was well underway.

There was still one problem, however — how to pay for construction. To finance the project, Pershing and the trustees agreed to sell $27,000 worth of bonds "payable in gold coin" and paying six percent annual interest. The bonds would be retired 10 to 15 years later beginning in 1920. Principal and interest would be payable through Kountze Brothers in New York City, the eastern branch of the family that controlled the Colorado National Bank. The town's credit must have been shaky, however. When the trustees voted to levy a tax to pay off the bonds, they made the ordinance "irrepealable." Even so, the town had to sell the bonds at a discount. Limon received only 91 cents on the dollar. (32)

Once constructed, the new system provided Limon with its first public water — but not enough water. In 1915, the board increased water rates 100 percent, set the meter rate on a consumption of up to 10,000 gallons per month, and authorized the superintendent to notify people wishing to use water for gardens that they would have to install meters or have their water turned off. That July, the town board approved a motion that "free water for lawns be withdrawn." (33)

People outside Limon soon began requesting hook-ups to the system. Rancher Porter Thompson made one such request. So, too, did many others. (34)

By 1917, however, it had become apparent that the waterworks, though but five years old, were inadequate. Operating costs were "excessive," concluded the board. The system "did not furnish adequate and sufficient fire protection" and was "defective" in other aspects. At the urging of A.N. (Abe) Christenson, a major force on the board, the town sold another $15,000 in bonds and hired Royal D. Salisbury, an engineer from Burlington, to expand the system. (35)

But water still remained short. Two years later in 1919, Christenson helped push through another $25,000 bond sale so that Salisbury could make even more "additions, extensions, and improvements" to the system. (36)

Although Salisbury's primary job was to run the waterworks, the trustees decided to expand his work — they gave him the task of providing the town electricity. He did that job well, too, and built Limon's first electric plant. But to run the new facility, the board appointed I.A. Rookstool the town's "electric inspector" and, to have "just and reasonable" rates, adopted a fee structure suggested by the Public Utilities Commission. (37)

Not everyone bothered to pay their electric bill on time. As a result, in January 1919, the board voted that "all electric current not paid for by the 10th of the month be turned off and not turned on till all arrearages are paid in full." Some businesses in town, such as the creamery, wanted "more power at less rates," but the board replied that this was "impossible." (38)

South Limon was not served by either water or electric lines. Its residents petitioned the board to extend service, and the trustees finally asked Rookstool to extend service. That only seemed fair given that the trustees already provided service to people on the outskirts of town. (39)

Another municipal problem was sewage. As the board announced, the town had "no sewer system or natural drainage" and the soil was "fast becoming permeated with corrupt matter and the air with offensive affluvia from cesspools and water closets, greatly endangering the lives and detrimental to the inhabitants." In December 1914, the board contracted with George H. Sethman of Denver, a "general engineer and constructor," to install "a sanitary sewer." After studying Limon's problem he estimated the cost at nearly $23,600, and the board quickly approved construction, "the cost to be assessed upon all the real estate" in the Limon Sanitary Sewer District #1. (40)

Although there may have been some opposition to building a sewer system, the project went forward in 1915. The town issued bonds to be paid off beginning twenty years later in 1935, if not called before. The board also asked for bids, and after consulting Sethman, awarded the contract to Gordon Taylor Construction Company of Denver. (41)

The work now went forward — but costs rose — and they rose past Sethman's "conservative" estimates. When workers completed the project late in the year, the cost of the system came to nearly $26,100, substantially more than estimates. Sethman explained the overage as resulting from interest, inspections, collection costs and incidentals, but not everyone seemed to be satisfied. (42)

Again, not everyone wanted to be in the Sewer District once it came on line. Zarelda LaForce, for one. The board referred her request to its attorneys in Denver. They advised the town that everyone in the district had to join and pay.

Defective workmanship soon appeared in some of the lines, and that had to be fixed as well. In the end, the system proved to have too little capacity. The board contacted Sethman again in 1920 to work on a sewer line extension for Limon. (43)

Recreation on the high plains — Limon's baseball park, 1908.

Walk's Camp grandstand was built by volunteers with donated lumber.

Bob Coulson Collection

The Great 1922 Limon Women's Tug of War. *Gloria Beedy Collection*

LIMON IN THE GREAT WAR

As Limon developed its public utility systems, there came the ominous rumblings of war in Europe. After nearly a century of relative peace, the continent plunged into what became known as the Great War or World War I in the summer of 1914. Three years later, in April 1917, the United States entered the battle as an "associated power" committed to the Allies — Britain, France, and Russia. President Woodrow Wilson led the American mobilization, and to command the million-man American Expeditionary Force dispatched to France, he appointed General John J. Pershing, a cousin of Limon's principal founder, William S. Pershing.

The Great War reached into Limon as it did every community in America. The pages of the Limon *Herald* told the story. In May 1918, the editors headlined: "Lincoln County Brain and Brawn to Fight the Hun" — "the Hun" being the way the press often characterized Germany. Elsewhere, the paper reported that the government had called draftees to report to Hugo, there to be entrained for boot camp at Deming, New Mexico, or Fort Logan in Denver. Among the boys going were Leo Haberthier, Clarence Einertson, and Harry Hubert Hockenberry. And there was more on the war effort in the *Herald's* columns. Limon had a garden club of 50 members which planned to do "something patriotic" to assist the war effort. The editors also announced that the Food Administration had regulated pinto bean production. (44)

The war dominated the news all year. In October 1918, the *Herald* published a plea from William G. McAdoo, the Director General of the Fourth Liberty Loan, asking the "railroad men" in the area, "officers and employees alike" to buy war bonds. "Lending your money to Uncle Sam is the finest use they can make of it...," declared McAdoo. "Now is the time for every fighting man in Europe and the industrial and financial army at home to go to the limit to make the great victories our soldiers have already won absolutely complete and final." Underscoring McAdoo's pleas was another headline, "Clarence Ford Again Wounded." There were few details. A cryptic government telegram had told Mrs. Ford that he was "seriously wounded," but little more. No one from Limon had been killed; the nearest war-related fatality was John J. Buhr of Hugo.

The editors liked to feature news of local "doughboys," the name given American soldiers in the war. The headline "Boys Go to U.S. Service," for example, carried the news that Murdo Urquhart, Chalmer Wells, and Edgar Jones had left for Fort Collins to enlist. Elsewhere there was a letter to a Mrs. Urquhart indicating that her son or husband (it wasn't specified) had left Camp Dix in New Jersey to make his way "across seas." And reports appeared that J.M. Grey, husband of Arbor Pershing Grey, was quite ill at Fort Leavenworth in Kansas. (45)

People at home did what they could to help. Mrs. Bernice Schlehuber "earnestly urged" each member of the Limon Branch of the American Red Cross to attend the annual meeting. The key subject would be Christmas packages to be sent to American soldiers abroad and sailors in home or foreign waters. "One parcel will be accepted by the War Department thru the Red Cross," she noted.

The *Herald* also published an article entitled "A Bit of Home with the Camp" — which referred to the activities of the YWCA (the Young Women's Christian Association). The group had established "hostess houses" at various posts for women visiting husbands and boyfriends. "Our boys are fighting for their homes," noted the article. Therefore, the YWCA was "helping to keep the ideal of the American home life constantly before the men who are protecting it. "

If there was anxiety about the war, there was also growing concern about the "Spanish Influenza" in Limon and elsewhere. The *Herald* reported that "every" schoolteacher in Boulder had become a house-to-house canvasser to ascertain the number of cases, the site of an "epidemic." There had been 30 deaths and 500 cases in Denver; 29 cases in Sterling. The Greeley City Council had closed "all schools, theaters, lodgerooms, billiard and pool rooms, and other places of public gathering." Cripple Creek had done the same. The editors noted Governor Gunter's proclamation calling for "stringent regulations to prevent spread of disease."

The flu, of course, swept the world. It may have killed more people than the war, and it impacted Limon. In 1918, in the mining town of Creede, it carried off William Stone and Finley Major Stone. With no means of support there, the two widows and their five children moved to Limon. Lola Stone found work at her father's store, the Hord Mercantile, where she worked till the late 1940s. Mabel Stone taught in the Limon schools. (46)

On the business front, there was news that Eva Schneider had purchased the Star Cafe from the Hockenberry Estate. "Miss Eva has good business experience," noted the editors, "and no doubt will have a good patronage in the future." The Kenega-Blair Hardware Company had reorganized as Kenega and Blair. The firm had increased its stock to include groceries and "the boys" expected to keep a bigger and better stock of hardware. Charles J. Schrader had one or two good dwellings for sale "on reasonable terms" and Mrs. Schrader wanted a buyer for an electric iron.

As for livestock, there was news of a "Large Lamb Shipment," which referred to Hamp Brothers shipping 1,750 animals on a special train, "the largest lamb shipment which has gone out of the county this year," noted the *Herald*. There was news of other cattle shipments from various ranchers. "The Karsh cattle were especially nice heavy steers," observed the editors.

Limon also had something of a labor shortage. School closed briefly that October, and Elizabeth Matzdorf, Helen Lundgren, and other women in town turned themselves into "farmerettes". Their job was to pull and stack beans. (47)

There was some news not related to the war. In October 1918, the *Herald* carried a photograph of U.S. Senator Lawrence C. Phipps, who was running for re-election as the Republican candidate. Elsewhere, there was news of local candidates ranging from Harvey C. Swinhart, who was running for Lincoln County Sheriff to Miss Lennie Beavers, who was campaigning for re-election as the county superintendent of schools. And on the front page was an extended obituary of Mamie Carrie Long, who had died suddenly at the age of 23. She had lived "a clean Christian life," intoned the editors.

Perhaps Limon's first auto race early in the automobile age.

AUTOMOBILITY

Even though Limon had emerged as a town that served the railroads, the rise of the automobile had a gradual, but ever larger impact, as the 20th century unfolded. Limon lay at the edge of a low escarpment that projected out across the plains. This topographical feature had made the community the natural place for the Rock Island's division point on the journey across the plains to Denver and Colorado Springs. As ever more cars appeared, that same feature made Limon the natural division point for automobile traffic.

As early as 1914, the town made an effort to use this feature to increase business. Abe Christenson got the town board to send delegates to the Goodroads Convention in Colorado Springs to see what could be done to improve Colorado's generally wretched dirt roads. The board also asked the county commissioners to provide financial support for the Pikes Peak Ocean to Ocean Race across Colorado. The route came through Limon. (48)

These efforts were a sign of the times. The automobile had come to stay, and Limon kept pace with the change. By 1920, the town had adopted its first ordinances to control traffic. It was now unlawful "to run, drive or operate any automobile, steam car, electric car, or any other conveyance" at more than 15 miles per hour within the town limits. It also became unlawful to drive "without head lights and tail lights burning." (49)

As motor traffic grew in the 1920s, the town expanded its role. The board eyed common carriers. In 1924, for example, it approved a request from Midwest Transit Company to operate a line through Limon, provided that it take out a regular truck license. The board increasingly dealt with the proliferating service stations that catered to the growing auto traffic on the high plains. By the mid-1930s, Limon prided itself as having 28 "filling" stations that served motorists bound across the region. (50)

Public health matters in town gradually fell into the hands of Dr. George A. Kennedy, Limon's leading physician. He took care of birth and death records,

Lincoln County's first gasoline truck, seen here in 1915.

and directed quarantines for whooping cough, measles, and other diseases, all in keeping with the medical practices of the day. He also apprised the trustees on various public health matters, notably conditions in the slaughterhouses west of town and on the many hog lots. (51)

Kennedy was the epitome of the small-town doctor. Everyone liked the tall, slender, affable physician who made his home and office in downtown Limon. Kennedy's upbeat personality masked a deep tragedy, however. His wife had become one of Limon's first automobile fatalities when she was thrown from her vehicle. Like many Limonites, Kennedy dined at the nearby Grier House, and there he met his second wife Wilhelmina, one of the Grier girls who served passengers on the trains.

Despite Limon's growth, animals still ran wild in the streets as late as the 1920s, and the trustees tried to deal with this issue. In October 1920, they passed an ordinance that "chickens be kept under fence and not allowed to run at large." This was expanded a few weeks later by another ordinance stating that "every owner, keeper, or person having in charge chickens, ducks, geese, or other fowl shall keep such...under a fence." They "shall not be permitted to run at large in the city limits." (52)

Garbage and trash created another problem. The trustees tried to deal with it via an annual spring clean-up. As early as April 1915, the town board called on the new mayor, P.O. Wells, who had succeeded Pershing, to issue "a clean up proclamation" that "all trash and etc." be piled in alleys to be hauled off at the expense of the town. (53)

Stranded travelers and transients generally termed "hobos" presented still another matter. The best solution seemed to be to provide them with food and passage out of town. In 1915, for example, the trustees reimbursed the Hotel Limon for providing meals to hobos. That was costly to a town generally strained for revenues, however, and even worse, the number of hobos increased. In 1917, the trustees met formally with the Rock Island's agent, J.T. Osborne, "to express their views regarding the handling of hobos." But the problem was beyond the town's control. The Big Sandy was noted for attracting hobos. After the afternoon freight train backed down to the lumber yards, so many hobos appeared that one resident said it often looked as if school had just let out. (54)

The automobile age only enhanced the "hobo" problem. Motorists sometimes ran out of money or otherwise found themselves stranded in Limon. As before, the town appropriated money to get them on their way. A.C. Sinclair, for example, received reimbursement for $1.64 in 1929 for "groceries + RR fare for tramp tourists." (55)

Grier Girls on the porch of the Grier House, one of 117 such establishments on the Rock Island line.

Probably related to the "hobo" problem were the goings-on in the town's bars and hotels which may have catered in part to a less than reputable element. In February 1918, the Methodist, Baptist, and Christian churches asked the trustees to close all the town's "pool halls, theatres, skating rinks, and other places on Sunday." This plea fell on deaf ears, however, although the board voted "to request" the closing of all places of amusement on Sundays. (56)

At least in public, Limon's mayors and trustees appeared to get along very well. Most votes on all issues were unanimous, but that probably obscured the bargaining and compromising that went on behind closed doors. But problems and personalities sometimes flared into public squabbles. In April 1919, the voters elected Pershing mayor once again. He immediately appointed various town officials, but when Christenson, Lamoreux, and others voted against his choices, Pershing abruptly resigned after just days in office. Apartment owner T.J. Bell became mayor. (57)

These internal problems continued. A year later, the voters elected Val Smith mayor. On the night he took office, however, Christenson, Lamoreux, and Mosher (half the board of trustees), stated that they could not serve under Smith, and they "conditionally" tendered their resignations. The fight apparently centered around Smith's appointment of the town treasurer, town clerk, and city engineer — the same offices that had compelled Pershing's resignation the year before. Wrangling followed for the next few weeks. In the end Christenson, Lamoreux, and Mosher all resigned from the board. (58)

Meanwhile, serious financial problems began to loom on Limon's horizon. In their effort to build public utilities and keep taxes low, the trustees had put off until tomorrow problems they didn't want to pay for in the short run — such as the water bonds sold to pay for the water system. The town had paid interest, but had made no provision to pay any of the principal. In November 1920, the trustees noted that the first payment on principal would be due on January 1, 1923, and thus they petitioned the State Tax Commissioner to increase the town's levies, "no provision heretofore having been made for the redemption of such issue." (59)

When that proposal went nowhere, in early December, the trustees decided on another approach — refinancing the debt. At its December 2 meeting, the board referred to issuing $30,000 in bonds, redeemable beginning in January 1921, scarcely one month away. But the board noted, "there are no funds in the treasury...and there will be none available for payment and redemption" beginning in January. Fortunately for Limon, the holder of the first 24 bonds consented to refunding, and the new bonds to be issued would mature between 1925 and 1940; the town agreed to set up a redemption fund and so passed an ordinance "for the immediate preservation of the public peace, health and safety, and an emergency is hereby declared...." (60)

Growing up in Limon in the 1920s seemed very simple compared to what it became in later years. It was "a typical small town," remembered Chuck Stone.

Limon's School, always a source of community pride, shows students in 1923.

"We kids played football and baseball in the streets or vacant lots." For entertainment in those days "we had the movies in the Auditorium Theatre. The movie house had only one projector, so that when a reel finished there was a small wait while another reel was threaded into the machine. And on Saturdays, we had the two-reel serial that left the hero in dire peril" — meaning that everyone would have to return next Saturday (and pay admission) to see how the hero or heroine managed to escape from his or her predicament. Chatauquas came to town about once a year. Churches sometimes had revivals. Everyone "knew it was noon when we heard the steam whistle from the Rock Island roundhouse." (61)

Children "had games," recalled Stone. "Run sheep run, kick the can, [and] ten-step football in which opposing groups of boys would gather in the street. We hardly ever were bothered by traffic, the football would be kicked and if caught by a member of the other team, the catcher took the longest ten steps he could and kicked it to the other end of the group, the object being to force the other team back. Lots of fun." But this game would be a casualty of the automobile age —" too much traffic." (62)

Children watch a fire at the Russell Gates Mercantile Company, 1926.

Winter sports were equally straight-forward. "The kids made their own entertainment," skating on the Big Sandy for one. "In the winter, we could skate on the creek through town, clear on down under the railroad track to what was called Pershing's Dam. It was really the sewer pond. We would stop at the town light plant and wash off our skates in the water cooling tower." Other times, kids would go cross-country skiing, building toboggans to use on the hills on the old road to Genoa, or go ice skating in the surrounding rural areas. (63)

High school sports attracted ever more attention in Limon. In 1930, Leonard Stenson came from Kansas to coach. Though remembered by one resident as "rough and tough," he put Limon football and basketball on the map and changed the school colors from brown and gold to black and white. "Old Stens" got what he wanted. Several years later, he was succeeded by Lloyd Gaskill, who made an enormous reputation as a coach. Band also grew in popularity, particularly under the leadership of "Scratch" Hunt. This musical excellence was to continue under the direction of Don Kimble, son of a pioneer family.

From time to time, various Limon groups sought to improve recreational opportunities. In June 1922, Mrs. I.A. Rookstool and Mrs. Fred Rice, representing the Delphian Club, questioned the town's inadequate "play ground fixtures" and asked the trustees "to assist in the erection of a slide." In 1925, the board agreed to allow the Landis Shows to provide a week's entertainment under the auspices of the Limon Baseball Club. (64)

The board also took care of public charity, voting to guarantee a Mrs. Thorp a $15 account in the stores to provide food until arrangements could be made with the county commissioners to supply her funds for same. (65)

Water remained a major concern in the community. In June 1920, the trustees contracted with Reid Construction Company of Denver to develop a new well. Later the board extended the water line to the Stanley Farm (the old Pershing Farm). But overall, water remained in short supply and consumed about half of the town's budget. In July 1924, the trustees approved drilling a number of test holes with a view to locating another well. The board also decided that all water users would have to install meters; the flat rate for usage would be abolished. A year later in 1925, the board hired Reid Construction Company of Denver to dig another well, which was completed by June and put "in first class condition." (66)

As the 1920s continued, the town had difficulty in collecting payment for the electric power it provided. In 1925, H.G. Wilkins, manager of the Equity Mercantile Association, which made flour, stated that the company could get lower electricity rates by installing its own plant; the town's rates were "prohibitive" and it would be impossible for them to continue in business if they could not get lower rates. But Equity was apparently representative of a larger problem. That November, the trustees acknowledged that the town had experienced "considerable trouble" in collecting delinquent accounts and advised the town clerk to inform all customers that their service would be discontinued if accounts were more than 30 days in arrears. (67)

The problem of collecting both water and electric bills intensified, however. Some residents seemed oblivious to threats to cut off their service for nonpayment. Even the Limon High School fell into arrears. In May 1926, the town notified all users that if they did not have meters connected by July 1, they would lose service. And former mayor T.J. Bell of the Bell Hotel went before the trustees to challenge a light and power bill for rooms, he said, were "practically empty all the time." (He got a $7.50 credit compensating for an "old mistake.") (68)

These two problems — the high cost of providing service and the endless frustration of collecting bills — came to a head in 1926. After what must have seemed like endless discussions, in early December, the trustees met with S. Sergeant Newberry, president of Commonwealth Utilities Corporation, along with a Mr. Durfee of the same company. Newberry and Durfee expressed the company's desire to buy both the electrical plant and the distribution system. In return, the trustees granted Commonwealth permission to send an engineer from Denver to inspect Limon's facilities. This work went favorably, and in March 1927, the board agreed to sell Commonwealth both the electrical plant and the distribution system subject to voter approval. On April 5, Limon's electorate approved the sale. Two days later, Commonwealth made the purchase and acquired a franchise to operate in Limon. To maintain continuity, I.A. Rookstool left the town's service and took the same position at the "C.U. Corp." (69)

Selling the electrical plant helped the town reduce its annual budget to $15,000, but did not end either the water shortage or the problem of collecting delinquent accounts. The trustees continued threatening to have the water commissioner cut off service to anyone in arrears. (70)

A Happy New Year at the Limon Shops! At the railroad's zenith, more than 300 people worked for the Rock Isand in Limon.

By the 1920s, Limon had grown to the point where it needed a larger, more permanent place to conduct business. In its early years, the town had rented space for public offices from its founder, William S. Pershing, but in the early 1920s, "city hall" had moved from place to place. This was clearly unacceptable.

In March 1923, the trustees scheduled a public vote to obtain approval to issue general obligation bonds that would be used to construct a building (for up to $7,500) that would be used for a town office, jail, and fire department. The balloting took place that April at "Pershing's Land Office...being the place of voting in said town," according to the legal notice. When the votes were counted, 133 people favored the town hall proposal; only 26 opposed it; one person submitted a blank ballot. (71)

The plans now went forward quickly. The board appointed an architect, a Mr. Redding from the firm of Redding and Son, an architectural enterprise in Denver. The contractor was selected (Griffith and Hickman for $8,954); so, too, were the subcontractors, mostly local people; and bonds were sold through a Denver firm. Limon's first town hall came into being in the course of 1923. (72)

To improve the town's appearance, the trustees also looked hard at public advertising. In the early 1920s, as automobile traffic proliferated, new signboards appeared all over Limon, much of it looked unsightly, but the town had no regulation. This situation led a group of the town's leading citizens, notably A.C. Sinclair, Val Smith, and May Harmonson, to petition the board to create a permit system, and to have all signs put up without such a permit removed as "a public nuisance." This, the board approved. (73)

Signboards, however, remained somewhat controversial — not so much because of their looks, but more because of their content. In 1929, the Limon branch of the Women's Christian Temperance Union (better known as the WCTU) along with the Nazarene Sunday School sent the board a resolution to abolish all billboards and posters advertising tobacco and cigarettes. Both groups also urged the board to enforce the laws regarding the sale of same to minors. But these petitions had little effect. All the board did was to ask the town clerk to take up the matter with the billboard companies — which meant that nothing was done. (74)

The Ellis Drug Store, where the great fire that nearly destroyed Limon began on January 1, 1924.

DISASTER

Although Limon grew steadily during the 1920s, disaster was not far away. The catastrophe came on New Year's Day — Tuesday, January 1, 1924 — with "the most disastrous fire that has ever befallen our city," declared the *Eastern Colorado Leader* in a special edition the day after the event.

In downtown Limon there was a drugstore owned by the firm of O.H. Ellis & Son. The building itself was a virtual billboard. A large sign for "ICE CREAM SODA" heralded the front door. A billboard on one side and a huge sign under the eaves on the other advertised that here was the "LIMON DRUG COMPANY". Under another cornice there was a sign proclaiming the "LAND OFFICE" of W.S. Pershing — "up stairs...cheap land...Limon Lots," it said. And for the town's smokers, the building made known that it had New York Havana Export Cigars. The signage that covered the Ellis building embodied everything that some people in Limon wanted to get rid of.

The fire started very quietly — in the flue coming from the furnace at the rear of the building. After a time, Dorothy Willson, a store clerk, saw smoke coming from the wall. She gave the first warning. Ellis himself, in the store at the time, threw a bucket of water at the wall and thought he had extinguished the blaze, but that was not so. Flames shot through the wall. Smoke poured into the room. Somebody sounded the fire alarm.

Firefighters now rushed to the scene. As smoke billowed into the air, they unrolled their hoses and shot streams of water at the building, but it did little good. The blaze had started between the walls and now engulfed the building. Calls went out for more water and more equipment. Soon the town had mobilized all its fire-fighting apparatus. The Rock Island Railroad put its own water supply into action, and firefighters soon had hose lines stretched from different parts of town.

With a stiff cold wind blowing across the plains, the fire proved hard to fight. As it spread, business people along the west side of Main Street rushed to get their goods out of the path of the flames. Townspeople turned out by hundreds, some to fight the fire, some to watch the excitement. Mayor Osborne and several trustees joined the firefighters. So, too, did Aubrey Leonard, a Rock Island passenger. Townswomen served hot coffee to the shivering and tired workers and helped remove goods from the buildings. As the hours passed, the situation remained tense. The wind continued to fan the flames, and the zero degree temperatures began freezing the clothes of the firefighters — some "freezing solid," reported the *Leader.*

Many people took "slippery chances" to prevent the fire from spreading. At one point, Milo Ivey, the town marshal, and A.C. Sinclair, president of the First National Bank, went into the Hord Store to work the nozzle of a hose. Just after they and others got out (the business hopelessly gone), the roof caved in. It was "pure luck," said the *Leader,* that they were not caught and burned to death.

Desperation grew as the hours passed. Ultimately, "when it was seen that the entire block would be gone if something drastic wasn't done," wrote the *Leader.* "Mayor Osborne ordered the wrecking of the building occupied by the Lundy Shoe Store." But even this desperate move seemed to have little impact.

Then came better luck. Shortly after townspeople had flattened the Lundy store, the wind changed direction. This, said the *Leader*, "probably did more than anything else to stop the rapid progress of the conflagration." Not until midnight, however, was the fire extinguished. Exhausted firefighters then trudged home to bed. By morning, the zero-degree temperatures had turned the dripping water into long slender icicles that glistened peacefully in the sun as they tapered off the charred embers of the buildings wrecked by the blaze.

The damage was extensive. The businesses destroyed included the Bell Clothing Company, the Ellis drugstore, Charley Hammond's rooming house above the drugstore, Hord's general merchandise, and the Lundy shoe store. Many other people experienced water damage, notably Dr. Kennedy the town's major physician, and former mayor Wells' loan company. The total loss was estimated at $150,000, although most of the business people had some insurance.

Narrowly avoiding destruction was the Carman Building, which housed the Modern Woodmen Lodge, the Rebekahs, the Royal Neighbors, the Knights of Pythias, and other clubs. They survived because the firefighters kept a stream of water on the roof and sides of the building.

The aftermath of the fire seemed almost anticlimactic. With the fire extinguished, Osborne ordered several men to watch the site to make sure the smoldering embers did not burst into flame. The town also put up a fence to close off the ruins. Several business people soon discovered some pilfering from the stocks moved into the city streets. To investigate the matter, Marshal Ivey and Deputy Sheriff I.A. Rookstool obtained several search warrants and ultimately arrested two individuals who were lodged in the town "bastille."

The Limon Volunteer Fire Department as it looked in 1912. Abe Christenson stands 6th from left, Val Smith, 7th from left, Both were prominent figures in Limon's history.

There may have been relief in Limon, but there was also criticism. The editors of the *Leader* had nothing but praise for the heroic efforts of the "valiant fire fighters," but overall, the *Leader* was somewhat critical of what had happened. "As is generally the case when there is no organization," said the paper, "there was more than one fire chief giving directions."

It could not be denied that Limon had had a close call. "Had it not been that the high wind changed its direction and finally ceased later in the day," observed the *Leader,* "we would have had another story to report, as the fire might have taken the entire business section and many of the residences."

In the end the *Leader* had nothing but praise. In fighting the fire, Limon had demonstrated that it had "an ample supply of water," which served as "conclusive proof that this is not a 'dry' farming country" (which was hardly true). Down at the power plant, Rookstool had kept the engines pumping water directly into the mains. The Rock Island also voluntarily pumped water via the substitute pumper (Ed Pershing). Yet at the same time, the *Leader* called for a "better organized department and some added equipment," such as a ladder that could reach the top of buildings.

Limon emerged from the fire in an optimistic frame of mind. The blaze was nothing more than "a temporary jolt," said the *Leader.* "The catastrophe" caused little hardship. The Hord company denied rumors it would not rebuild. Instead, the owners declared they would hold a "fire sale," slash prices, and clean up inventory. The town began clearing the ruins. And the *Leader* announced the fire would be remembered as little more than an "inconvenience." "It takes more than a fire to take the 'Mon' out of Limon," declared the editors. "Tuesday's fire means a Bigger and Better Limon." (75)

LIFE IN THE 1920s

Some things in Limon seemed not to change — such as liquor sales. The 1920s were a time of prohibition — when the manufacture, sale, and consumption of alcoholic beverages of all types was unconstitutional — but that apparently mattered little in Limon and just about everywhere else in America. People made what they wanted and sold what they could. Limon was little different. The local branch of the WCTU took notice and persuaded the town board to pass a new ordinance relating to "intoxicating liquors," but that had little effect. If you wanted a drink, there was little problem. (76)

As was the case earlier, trash remained a challenge, particularly in the spring, and Limon dealt with the problem in pretty much the same way. In 1927, the town designated the week of June 6-11 "Clean Up Week," a time to get rid of rubbish which had become a fire hazard. The trustees had "a dodger" with instructions delivered to every house. In 1928 came a novel idea. The Boy Scout Committee asked the trustees that the scouts be allowed to clean up the trash as the scouts were "badly in need of uniforms and equipment." That brought a favorable response. The board agreed to pay the scouts $1.00 for each load of rubbish and trash. (77)

The Boy Scouts couldn't do much about junk cars. In the late 1920s, the trustees received "a number of complaints" about junks stored on vacant lots around town — so many complaints that the vehicles finally were "considered a nuisance." Some abandoned junks may have been owned by the two automobile companies in town — the Harris Motor Company and the Spaid Motor Company. The town finally notified the firms to move these cars out of the city limits or haul them to the dump. When nothing happened, the town ordered the cars removed under the nuisance ordinance. (78)

Until the late 1920s, men dominated all the elective and appointive offices in town. Women signed various petitions and voted in elections, but in terms of political life, their sphere was limited to one activity. They generally comprised the election judges — and those who served were generally the wives of either elected or appointed officials. This, however, began to change in the late 1920s when Veva Foe was appointed town treasurer. (79)

A heavy snowstorm blankets the high plains, making Limon a haven for stranded motorists.

Limon merchants sought to stimulate the economy during the Great Depression. Here in the 1930s, the Smithburg family from nearby Genoa, won the drawing for a new Chevrolet.

The Great Depression

The Great Depression of the 1930s hit Limon as hard as it did any community in the United States. As economic conditions grew steadily worse, the Rock Island Railroad cut back on employment and reduced "its yard, shop, and road forces to a minimum." The Limon National Bank failed — a huge blow to rancher Porter Thompson, one of its major investors. Many small firms saw their business slide, and farmers and ranchers around town could do nothing about slumping prices. (80)

The town's government saw its problems begin to mount, often in subtle ways. There were ever more complaints about water charges. In July 1930, for example, A.C. Sinclair complained that his water bill was "excessive." Dr. G.A. Kennedy objected to paying the town $10 "for thawing frozen pipes in his office." As problems grew, the trustees reduced charges to individuals and enterprises like the Equity Mercantile Association, and as more individuals refused to pay bills for having their pipes thawed, the board voted to waive such balances. (81)

Water users outside Limon had less clout, however. When Porter Thompson objected to his bill, the board was unmoved. In fact, in 1931, as revenues dwindled, the town increased rates 50 percent to outside users. Out-of-towners howled in protest, so much so that the board finally bowed to pressure and reduced rates slightly, in part because those living outside town had to install and maintain their own pipes. (82)

But as the Depression mounted, getting people in Limon to pay their bills became a chronic problem. "Water bills were not being paid as promptly as usual," noted the trustees in February 1931. "Numerous notices" had been sent to

An early aerial view of Limon, Colorado, showing the growing town and the railroad yards.

different users, but with "little success toward collection." The trustees directed the water supply be turned off to delinquent people, but that did little good. Soon the town began losing $100 per month for delinquent water users alone. (83)

It was not only water bills. People also refused to pay the dog tax — and the board told the clerk to haul nonpayers into court. Residents like Charles Kempf put up a "drink stand" on the parking space in front of his home. He refused to remove it even when confronted by the night marshal. That led to another stand in front of the Cope-Kennedy Filling Station. In 1931, the board hauled eight boys, who had not paid fines for "wreckless driving" and other infractions, into court in order to collect payment. (84)

By 1931, the Depression's impact could be seen in plans for the town's annual Christmas lighting. In previous years, I.A. Rookstool of Commonwealth Utilities had not only provided electricity for Christmas lights but also furnished and installed the bulbs for $175. This year, he offered to do the work for $100 if the town would furnish a man to do the job. But the financially pinched trustees rejected even that offer. Instead, they offered just $75 "toward xmas lighting" in Limon. "If the merchants wanted the lights," resolved the board, "they should put up the balance." The board also considered an offer from Scott Decorating to provide the town with Christmas trees for unemployed workers to sell. (85)

Commonwealth Utilities itself seemed to be getting into trouble. Early in 1932, Limon found itself without electric lights for five hours, in part, it appeared, because the company had failed to do proper maintenance and had let its plant run down. Years later, in 1942, the newly incorporated Mountain View Electric Association acquired Commonwealth. (86)

Affairs in town got so bad that in March 1932, the board had to recognize that with no tax money being collected, it could not even pay its own bills. That situation was rectified later in the month. (87)

The Depression even caused problems in making payments! Limon paid interest due on its water bonds through Kountze Brothers in New York. When that firm failed in the growing crisis, the town treasurer informed the board that the $265 sent to pay interest due on the bonds had not been paid. To recover the money, the trustees authorized the treasurer to join a group seeking a preferred position in claims owed by Kountze Brothers. (88)

As the crisis unfolded, Limon seemed to run down. One person who moved to town in 1936 remembered that it was "not an attractive place to live: the Dust Bowl days, the Depression, tumble weeds blowing down Main Street. The area was plagued by jack rabbits and grasshoppers." (89)

The Depression affected the plans of many people — like those of Chuck Stone. He came home from the University of Colorado at Christmas one year. "The money had run out," he said. Stone went to work in the family-owned Hord Mercantile and helped build a slaughterhouse on the Porter Thompson Ranch. He also tried to collect unpaid bills. He and Jim Fleming, the manager of Hord Mercantile, "would go out in the country and try and get a steer or a calf from a farmer that owed the store a bill that they couldn't pay." (90)

It became hard to get credit — few banks wanted to loan money for fear they would not be repaid. To buy a red Chevrolet from Spaid Motor Company in 1936, Jack Grenawalt made a down payment from inventory in his father's store. (91)

The devastating Memorial Day Flood of 1935 destroyed entire towns and necessitated rebuilding Rock Island bridges and trackage over a wide area. *Kosley Collection*

Yet the Depression affected different generations in different ways. For children, the Depression did not seem like hard times — they had never known anything else. For adults, it was far different. The Depression, said one survivor, "created a way of life" that remained with them for the rest of their lives. (92)

In April 1932, a new board came into being. The new mayor was former mayor J.T. Osborne, the Rock Island agent in town. The new board of trustees consisted of both new and old faces, including Abe Christenson and A.C. Sinclair. With the nation, the state, and the town itself now slipping toward the abyss of the Depression, the new board decided on drastic action. That meant reducing Limon's budget, part of which would come through cutting the salaries of town employees. Water Commissioner Fred Foe saw his salary reduced 33 percent from $150 to $100 per month. The clerk's salary was cut in half. Only the town marshal managed to retain his regular pay. (93)

Osborne and the new trustees found another innovative way to reduce costs. That was to cut the wattage in the town's light bulbs. By reducing the number of watts from 100 to 60, the town could save 80 cents per bulb per month. Every penny counted in the crisis. (94)

Given the struggle to make ends meet, it came as no surprise to anyone that Osborne and his colleagues reduced future town budgets as the 1930s limped forward. Planned expenditures stood at $14,500 for 1932, but Osborne and company reduced that to $11,500 for the fiscal year beginning in April 1933. (95)

It was one thing to cut costs and budgets, but there was also the question of increasing revenues insofar as possible. The trustees recognized that many

The stately Masonic Temple on Limon's E Avenue was built in 1919. The Masons, Eastern Star, Odd Fellows, and Rebekahs had a significant influence on town development.

people in town had not complied with the ordinance to install water meters, and so the board authorized Osborne to investigate each case personally, along with Commissioner Foe, and make sure that everyone had them installed. Osborne also petitioned the county commissioner to grant Limon $12.50 to $15 per month to buy gasoline and other necessities for travelers who were stranded in town. He himself petitioned the board to refund him money expended "for charitable purposes." (96)

The trustees also discussed unemployment in town. They thought they might employ some people on the county roads going through town, then realized that the county commissioners handled that matter completely and decided to refer anyone seeking employment on the roads to them. (97)

Limon's first depot, serving both the Rock Island and Union Pacific, and the Grier House (on the right), were much anticipated stops on the busy train schedule.

The Depression also effected public health regulation. Small, licensed dairymen who delivered milk and other products into town wanted the trustees to either enforce or abolish the license fee because some hard-pressed dairymen were selling milk without a license. Dr. Kennedy, the town's public health officer, not only confirmed the practice, but also concluded that "very few" producers were in compliance. When confronted with the problem, Osborne and the other trustees reaffirmed Limon's commitment to regulating dairies and deliveries because of the health issues involved. They directed Kennedy to issue licenses and bring everyone into compliance within 60 days. But that proved easier said than done in hard times. Kennedy had only limited success. Given the situation, in December, the trustees refunded the fee that some had paid. Then on Christenson's suggestion, to start anew, they had the town's attorney, Frank Safranek, develop a new licensing arrangement. (98)

Dairy producers were not the only ones to oppose licensing. Coal dealers in Limon complained that truckers came into town and sold fuel without a license. To deal with the matter, the board adopted an ordinance like one in Salida which required all those selling coal to be licensed. Fuel was only one source of complaint. Limon's merchants protested "against the peddlers of produce and food stuff" and "had about the same grievance as the Coal Dealers." In this case, the trustees reviewed a Cañon City ordinance in hope of addressing the merchants' concerns. (99)

As the Depression continued, its impact could still be seen in nonpayment for water. Ethel Evans, a property owner in town, notified the board that she would not be responsible for any future water bills at the C.W. Leeman property. Some

As auto traffic increased dramatically, the Cozy Cafe in downtown Limon became one of the most famous restaurants on the high plains.

people went to greater lengths. The board authorized the installation of meters in houses that had never had them — and began cutting off water for noncompliance. That was now an old story. Some residents simply defied the city, such as A.D. Clausson. He allegedly yanked out his water meter and installed his own pipe in the system. That kind of action prompted tough talk by the board, but results didn't change. Evading water payments had become epidemic, and the trustees had to acknowledge that "numerous water users" were delinquent. (100)

Some hard-pressed residents turned to the trustees for help. A Mrs. Williams told the board that she had used her $7 in federal aid; and that she and her children were now out of food. When the board advised her that the County Commissioners would take care of her at the County Poor Farm, she declared that she did not care to go that route. As a result, Mayor Osborne authorized the town clerk to give her a $1.00 food voucher good at E.L. Williams's store. (101)

Despite the continuous nonpayment, water consumption in Limon increased during the Depression. In 1931, the trustees approached Reid Construction about digging a new well, but nothing could be done in the immediate future. In June 1932, however, the problem became serious. Water Commissioner Foe reported that the town's supply was getting low, and he thought it necessary to restrict consumption to ensure that the town would have enough water come summer. To study the problem, the mayor appointed a committee. It suggested that digging a trench between the town's two existing wells seemed like a "plausible" way to increase supplies. Foe, however, would not be in charge of this project. The board fired him on a 3-2 vote in September, with no reason stated. (102)

Like the ongoing problems with water, some things in town never changed. Some groups protested about entertainment on Sunday, but the Auditorium Theatre stayed open. Junk yards and junk cars despoiled many lots, and new junk dealers made the problem even worse. (103)

The old hobo problem intensified. Local residents gave these homeless people food and water, but could not help those who wanted work. The hobos slept close to the railroad tracks, and their campfires, where they perked coffee in old metal pots, remained a fond memory for some residents. The sight of the hobos jumping the freight trains to move to another town also seemed to many a mysterious adventure.

Most communities in America experienced problems like Limon's, but what intensified the Depression on the high plains were the dust storms. They compounded the impact of hard times in Nebraska, Kansas, Oklahoma, Eastern Colorado, and elsewhere. The dust storms reflected both poor agricultural practices that stripped off the topsoil and the advent of a dry cycle due to the lack of rain. Limon did not escape. It lay at the western edge of America's now-notorious Dust Bowl.

Dust storms swirled across the high plains all around Limon. Margaret Vermillion remembered years later that "crops dried up [and] grass was scarce for our milk cows." But living on a farm, they never went hungry. They had pigs and chickens along with milk, cream, butter, eggs, and produce from the garden. "But the dust was terrible." (104)

Everyone remembered the dust. "Huge black clouds of dust," noted Chuck Stone. "No matter how tight the windows there was always about a quarter of an inch of fine dust on the window sill inside." Jack Grenawalt once found he was unable "to see across E Avenue because of the dust." (105)

The dust storms had a huge impact on travel. One woman reflected years later that the storms were "just a way of life," but she also recalled "going to Denver and waiting hours to be able to drive on." Another individual observed that "the dust storms would engulf one's car until you could not see the radiator ornament," and you could sit for some time before being able to see to drive." The dust sometimes buried the fences along the road.

The dust affected home life as well. Some people found that the winds were so strong it was impossible to have a fire at home. Others burned kerosene lamps during the day to provide light for their rooms. And any number of families hung wet sheets over their windows to keep out the dust. (106)

The storms altered life in the schools. One teacher found that the dust made it so dark in her room that students couldn't see enough to read; she invented a game similar to croquet so that the students would "spend most of the time on the floor under the protection of the desks" until the winds abated near sundown and parents could come to pick up the children. (107)

Even as the Depression intensified, Limon still had one growth industry — gas stations. During the 1930s, the trustees received more and more applications to install gas pumps and open service stations. This reflected the continuing growth in automobile travel and the construction of new roads, such as U.S. Highways 24 and 40, which intersected in Limon. By the end of the decade, the town had more gas stations than any other community of comparable size in the country. Limon even appeared in *Ripley's Believe It or Not* for this. (108)

At its peak, Limon's Main Street had 28 gas stations to serve the traveling public.

The Auto Service Building, another Limon landmark, stood next to the Cozy Cafe on Main Street.
Kruplak Collection

WORLD WAR II

As the Depression ground on year after year with no end in sight, the world was nonetheless plunging down the road into global conflict again. Rumblings of war emerged in the late 1930s in both Europe and Asia. Finally, on September 1, 1939, Nazi Germany invaded Poland, and the globe erupted into history's most devastating conflict — World War II. The United States began to rearm, which soon ended the Depression. Then it began to aid the western allies, notably Great Britain, and tried to restrain the Japanese war machine in East Asia by cutting off Japan's supply of oil and other strategic materials.

To obtain the materials it needed, the Japanese government decided to expand the war. Fearing intervention by the United States, the Japanese chose a preemptive strike to destroy the United States Pacific Fleet at Pearl Harbor in Hawaii. The attack came early on the morning of December 7, 1941. Aircraft from six Japanese aircraft carriers northwest of Hawaii struck Pearl Harbor at 7:55 a.m. They caught the navy totally by surprise. In minutes, the bombers, torpedo planes, and fighters wreaked havoc. They destroyed two battleships and other smaller warships, and they damaged other battleships and lesser craft. They also destroyed many aircraft on the ground. At least one Limon man was there —Louis W. Menge, an army air force mechanic stationed at Hickam Field. He was wounded in action while helping to get planes out of the hangar during a strafing attack. For his "conspicuous gallantry," he was given the opportunity to go to officer's candidate school and eventually became a B-17 bomber pilot. (109)

Pearl Harbor was one of the most psychologically shattering events in American history. For the rest of their lives, people remembered exactly where they were when they heard the news. It was no different in Limon. "Driving home from Genoa when the announcement came over the radio," recalled Irma Kjosness. "Eating dinner with my parents," said Gladys Lusk. "On a ladder at the front of the house putting up Christmas lights," noted Chuck Stone, whose wife Winnie rushed out with the news. At Karval, where she and her husband went into a store after hunting rabbits, wrote Norma Grenawalt. (110)

And the reaction to what President Roosevelt would call a day of "infamy"? "Disbelief," said one person. "Fear and sadness," remembered another. "Fear," wrote a third. "Anger," said another. "Just could not comprehend," stated another. "Stunned, my throat went dry," recalled another driving home with her husband from Genoa. "I don't think we spoke the rest of the way home." (111)

World War II quickly did what Roosevelt's New Deal had not. It put people to work, ended the Depression, and restored prosperity (even if wartime shortages meant that few had a place to spend the money).

The railroad industry surged ahead. In Limon, the Rock Island hired many new people, including some men it had discharged during the Depression (if they were still in the area). Before long, road crews became hard-pressed to keep up with the number of trains rumbling across the high plains with troops and war material of all description. (112)

The upsurge in traffic brought changes and opportunity. Enterprising teenagers like Jim Statton and Don Morrison (who grew up to become long-term Limon entrepreneurs) waited for the passenger and troop trains to arrive, then went on board to sell newspapers to news-hungry travelers. Soldiers sometimes cheered from the windows of pullman cars as the troop trains pulled out of town. And later in the war, came the heavily guarded prisoner-of-war trains which stopped briefly, sometimes so that J.O. Clanin, one of Limon's physicians, could go aboard to treat the sick.

As the nation mobilized fully in 1942, there were appeals of all sorts to support the war effort. Salvage drives were very popular — scrap metal was in huge demand. Schools conducted drives to get all the used metal. Other organizations appealed to the community. "Tin Can Salvage Depot now at old *Leader* Office," headlined the *Leader* in February 1944. The paper also printed encouraging words from Mrs. Harry Lawson, salvage chairman.

Since raising money was essential, war bond drives became a part of life. A.N. Christenson, now in the oil business, took a leading role in one. Limon's former mayor A.C. Sinclair served as co-chair of Lincoln County's Fourth War Loan Drive, which raised more than $295,000, far ahead of the county's quota in the statewide campaign. Even the town itself purchased bonds. (113)

Aside from the drives, rationing of just about everything quickly became a major part of everyone's life. Rationing was followed very strictly. There were no new cars, vehicles, or machinery. It was hard to get enough gas. It became nearly impossible to get even so much as a tire unless you had an old one for trade. (114)

Food rationing became part of life — you had to get food stamps to obtain what you needed. Sugar and coffee were the most desirable of the restricted products, but families worked together and often shared stamps. Meat was always in short supply. *The Limon Leader* tried to help there. On one occasion it headlined "6 Stew-pendous Ways to Stretch Meat Rations" — then featured an article with recipes replete with a cartoon. Overall, food supplies in Limon were not quite as restricted as elsewhere. Some farmers produced enough for themselves and gave away their meat and butter stamps. (115)

People in Limon, like Americans elsewhere, were philosophical about the situation. Despite the privations, said one, "we were safe and did not suffer from shortages." The war itself was uppermost on their minds. They had "lots of anxiety about the progress of the war." (116)

It was obvious from the outset that the war would have a huge impact on individual lives. Margaret M. Vermillion "cried all day" when she heard the news of Pearl Harbor. It seemed likely that her boyfriend would have to enter the service, which would disrupt their plans to be married. The attack that Sunday morning meant that they didn't know what to do or what would eventually happen. Ultimately, they decided to marry in January before he entered the Army Air Force. (117)

Margaret Vermillion's thoughts foreshadowed much of what happened to young men and women in Limon in the four years ahead. The war quickly scattered them all over the world — and to places hardly anyone had ever heard of before.

The war split young families. When Chuck Stone was sent to Hawaii, he had to leave his wife Winnie in Limon "to contend with all the rationing and the shortages." The same went for Jack Grenawalt. He spent two years in India while his wife Norma and their infant son remained in Limon. With most of its young men gone to war, Limon seemed "a community of older men and women." (118)

If the war took people away, it also brought others together. Individuals who would not have met otherwise found spouses in California, North Carolina, Tennessee, and a host of places far from the plains where they had grown up. (119)

With the manpower shortage, some women from Limon found work in defense industries. Gladys Lusk "learned to drive a tractor and help on the farm." Mary Garnhart became a cashier at the Pueblo Army Air Base. (120)

Women also joined the armed services. Beverly Larson signed on with the WAVES, which was part of the Navy. After training, she was sent to New Orleans, Louisiana, to help direct naval air traffic. Margaret Leeman, daughter of Limon's town clerk, became the first woman from Lincoln County to join the Women's Auxiliary Army Corps, best known as the WACs. She was ordered to Fort Des Moines, Iowa. Later, WAC recruiters came to Limon and enlisted Mazie Sutton, a schoolteacher, and Zelma Bowling Moorhead, a former student. (121)

Despite the frustrating shortages and the worries about who might and who might not return, there was a lighter side to the war. *The Limon Leader* often caught this in the columns of a weekly feature called "SOSAMAIA." Here the editors published short vignettes about where Limon's sons and daughters had migrated and what they were doing. Beverly Larson, for one, reported that the only thing inconvenient about her job in New Orleans was that the barracks weren't finished and she had to stay at a hotel 20 miles away. Private E. E. "Jiggs" Jenkins, formerly of the *Leader* staff, sent the editor a bunch of Japanese propaganda leaflets from New Guinea. C.L. McCorkle, who was in the Merchant Marine, reported that he served way "down in the engine room of a tanker, which is an ideal place not to be." And Corporal Fred Garnhart wrote that he did not get seasick sailing to England; "The English villages are very clean," he wrote, "but oh, how very black the blackouts are." (122)

By the 1940s, Limon had finally developed tree-lined streets—a fond memory for servicemen.

Many soldiers and sailors thought of home. Sergeant Gene Oliver, a bombardier weary of England's rain, wished he was in Limon to enjoy the snow. Junior Steele, stationed in New Caledonia in the South Pacific, wrote home about how terribly hot it was and how he longed for a Colorado snowstorm; he "would wade out in snow up to my knees," and, "maybe get cooled off again." (123)

E Avenue in Limon, ca. 1940. The Houtz Drug on the left was site of the 'draw-a-name' program.

The Limon Leader, spurred in part by Helen Christenson, took the lead in keeping Limon's faraway soldiers, sailors, and airmen in touch with home through a project later covered in *The Reader's Digest* magazine. The editors did this with a "draw-a-name" program down at the Houtz Drug. The *Leader* put the names of all the men and women from Limon serving in the armed forces into a bucket shaped like a tipi, urged townspeople to draw a name, and "write to this person, send him remembrances on his birthday anniversary and upon holidays." Mail call is "the most important one in the armed forces," noted the editors; "you should do your part to see that no one is disappointed. This should be one of your contributions towards winning the war."

The results were positive. In December 1943, Dale Gifford wrote from Italy that he was "very happy" to receive the "greeting letter from the folks in Limon.... It was something I'm sure that none of the fellows in my company have received, and I had never seen anything like it." Sergeant Bill Bertram, who was also stationed in Italy, wrote the *Leader* that his letters made him "a bit of homesick, but it means a lot to a fellow to know he isn't forgotten." Limon stayed in touch. (124)

Even for those at home in Limon, the war was not that far away. Colorado was an important training center and the eastern plains sometimes a bombing area. The headlines and stories in the *Leader* occasionally brought news of crashes — some close to home. "Liberator Plane Crashed South of Hugo Friday," headlined the paper in January 1944. The article told the sad story of how a midwinter snowstorm had prevented the B-24 bomber from landing along the Front Range and how it had run out of fuel over Hugo. Everyone parachuted. Two men died; three others landed safely. (125)

Limon sustained its share of the casualties, and the columns of the *Leader* brought the gut-wrenching news. "Son of Limon Woman Reported to be Japanese War Prisoner," ran one headline in 1943, which referred to Mrs. Neva Bates, who had recently moved to town and who now had to deal with the report that her son, Arthur Lee Bates, had been taken prisoner in the Philippines.

In March 1944, the crowd at the Limon High basketball game was stunned into silence when it was announced over the loudspeaker that Tommy Sinclair was missing in action. The next issue of the *Leader* carried more news. Next to the same column noting former mayor Sinclair's successful war loan campaign was the ominous headline: "Capt. Tommy Sinclair Reported Missing After Mission from Air Base in India." Captain Sinclair flew what they called "the Hump," a difficult transport route used to supply British and Chinese forces in Southeast Asia. Later the news improved. After many anxious days came the report that Sinclair had been found alive. He had been forced to parachute into the jungle when one of his engines failed. (126)

There were others, too. Boatswain's Mate Delbert R. "Junior" or "Doc" Steele, who fought in several major naval battles in the Pacific, was severely burned and temporarily lost his sight in both eyes when his ship was torpedoed in the South Pacific in 1944. Bill Bertram was wounded in Italy early in 1944, though he wrote home that "it didn't amount to anything." Fred Pfleeger was also wounded in Italy — serious leg wounds, he reported. And so was the *Leader*'s former employee — "Jiggs Jenkins Wounded," headlined the *Leader* in November 1944 — although Jenkins later wrote that it was all a mistake.

Some, of course, did not come back. "Son of Limon Woman Is Killed in Action," headlined the *Leader* in April 1943. Which referred to Sergeant Gene Smith, the son of Mrs. T.W. Moyer of Limon; he was a bombardier on a B-17 Flying Fortress shot down over Germany in March 1943. Then several months later came another grim headline, "Joey Johnson Killed in North African Action." The article told of Private Johnson's life and his death in Sicily.

Some deaths occurred in training accidents. Elmer Murphy, once a popular schoolteacher in Limon, died in a B-24 Liberator crash near Omaha while helping test the airplane. Jim Wakefield died in a training flight in New Jersey.

It was the air war, so vital to the Allied war effort, that seemed to claim many connected to Limon. Lt. Kenneth Foe, a bombardier who had grown up in town, died in the skies over Germany after more than 20 combat missions. So, too, did another flyer, Lt. K.R. (Bobby) Kessinger, grandson of Dr. and Mrs. J.D.

Bernard Kollath, far left, on leave with Army buddies in Montreux, France, near the end of World War II. *Kollath Collection*

Kessinger, who was also shot down over Germany. And there was Lt. Louis Menge, who had survived the attack at Pearl Harbor, only to be shot down over Romania in 1944. Still another pilot was Lt. Richard C. Allison, who grew up in Limon, killed over Peleliu Island in the South Pacific the same year. (127)

Despite the privations, the rationing, and the jolting news from the battlefronts, some semblance of normal life still went on in Limon. The town board sold more bonds to finance repairs and expand the sewer system — and had problems paying the contractors. Weeds grew tall on vacant lots and unpaved streets. Private trash burning became a real fire hazard. The trustees held various discussions about public health — notably the problems caused by garbage and rats — the solution to which was removing the garbage from alleys and piles. To that end, trustees Charles Kennedy and Dale Cooley were appointed a committee of two "to see that all garbage was cleaned from the alleys and back of buildings." (128)

There were other somewhat routine matters. In 1944, the trustees deemed the old Lincoln Hotel "unsafe for occupancy and a fire hazard." So as a matter of "public safety," they voted to condemn the structure and have it removed. There were many discussions about "oiling" — or paving — the streets. In November 1944, as the year-end approached, Mr. and Mrs. Louis Milano asked the trustees to have the water turned off for the winter in the old Limon Filling Station because the pipes often froze and, when thawed, the water released flooded their home. (129)

The war prompted Limon's two political groups, the Taxpayers Party and the Citizens Party, to put their jousting aside for awhile and form common cause. Early in 1944, the year for local elections, the Taxpayers Party nominated a slate headed by Mayor Frank E. Ainsworth. The Citizens Party endorsed the same slate. With the result preordained, the town board debated whether or not to hold municipal elections at all, but in the end the voting went forward on schedule that April. Mayor Ainsworth stayed in his post, the only change being that Charles Wheeler replaced old Tom Cope, the garage owner, as trustee, as both parties had previously agreed. (130)

Camp Pershing, built in 1937 on East Main Street, also included a gas station and restaurant to serve Limon's growing tourist traffic.

Postwar Years

As World War II ended in 1945, many throughout the United States predicted the nation would slip back into the trough of depression. But that prediction proved wrong. By 1945, the populace had endured more than 15 years of deprivation from the Great Depression and World War II combined. Goods of all sorts, from cars to clocks, had worn out, and that spurred a huge postwar demand for consumer products of every kind. Those 15 years of hardship had also retarded family formation; the postwar result was an unprecedented and unforeseen "baby boom." Finally, the great coalition that had won the war quickly fell apart in peacetime. In its place came the Cold War, which would last for the next half century and prompt a huge peacetime military buildup. Instead of a return of the Great Depression, the postwar years unleased a nationwide economic boom.

The Limon Town Hall, built in 1923 at a cost of $8,954, provided space for town offices, jail, and fire department. *Kruplak Collection*

In the Limon area, this boom had mixed results. The number of people engaged in agriculture steadily declined in the postwar years. Lincoln County saw its rural population decline substantially from 1940 to 1950. And the railroad industry saw its star fade as well, eclipsed by the shift to cars, trucks, and airplanes.

The changes in agriculture seemed slow and subtle. The *Leader* reported on agricultural developments — a new farm cooperative in Limon, new Beefmaster cattle on the Lasater Ranch near Matheson, exceptional wheat yields on local farms, local cowboys winning rodeo events, and the organization of the Cowbelles for women involved in cattle raising. Farmers remained worried about more grasshopper infestations like those that plagued the area in the late 1930s. Some rural people moved into Limon or other towns. The Nicks Brothers, who had operated the Hillside Dairy for years, put their cattle up for auction and departed the business. Abe Christenson, who had owned the town's pioneer bulk operator plant since 1915, quit the business after 37 years. The federal government announced that it had changed the name of agriculture in the region from "dry land" farming to "high plains" farming, but that hardly concealed the reality of decline. Sure enough, the 1950 census revealed that Lincoln County's rural population had declined 15 percent from 5,882 people in 1940 to 4,955 people in 1950. (131)

The same decline could be seen on the railroad. Once the war ended, the Rock Island experienced a lull in its business. As the postwar boom took hold, the line's traffic rose substantially, but this was only temporary. The postwar years saw the railroad industry engulfed in problems — most notably, the enormous

The Limon depot, shown in 1950, became the last survivor of the town's railroad heyday. In the 1990s it housed the Limon Heritage Museum.

competition that came from cars, trucks, and airplanes. The change was soon felt by the railroad workers in town. By the mid-1950s, the Rock Island had cut back its operations in Limon to the point where the yards and shops were only a semblance of their old selves. The roundhouse was torn down and replaced for a time by a diesel house. One by one, many of the buildings and structures associated with the railroad were razed. Eventually, all that survived was the Limon depot. (132)

Yet the Rock Island line still brought attention to Limon. The Rocky Mountain Rocket was a famous train and Limon the division point for service to and from Denver and Colorado Springs. Each afternoon, the silver, red, and maroon diesel

With an eye to the future, the Chamber of Commerce began to advertise Limon as the "Hub City of Eastern Colorado." *Dan Houtz Photo Collection*

would arrive from Denver with its silver cars to link up with the Colorado Springs diesel section pulled by the unique, squared-end AB6 units. The sleek diesel from the Denver section would be put ahead of the special AB6, the baggage cars and pullmans interlinked, all in the course of about 15 minutes, then the train dispatched on its thousand-mile run to Chicago. Westbound Rockets arrived in Limon about 6:30 in the morning, to be broken down quickly into the two sections bound for Denver and Colorado Springs.

In the 1950s, Limon also became noted when the Rock Island appointed Anna McGowan one of the nation's few women yardmasters. This was the culmination of a 40-year career that "Miss Anna" pursued on the railroad.

If agriculture and railroading developed problems in the postwar years, there was good news elsewhere. Exploration for natural gas had begun a few miles north of Limon at Last Chance. The source of the town's electrical power switched from Colorado Springs to Brush. (133)

The economy also seemed to be changing locally. Limon obtained a Piggly Wiggly store in 1947, a sign that here, too, the national supermarket chains were about to supercede the local grocery stores. Lloyd Gaskill, Limon's noted football coach, was planning to open Gaskill's Clothing Store. The town hoped to get on the national weather map because a weather station was established at the Bell residence in northeast Limon. Reports would go to Denver every three hours

A Rock Island snowplow works its way across the plains near Limon.

Lois Scott Collection

and become part of the United States Weather Service. Finally, in 1952, Limon got its first telecast — all the way from Atlanta, Georgia — as the great postwar TV phenomenon began to penetrate the high plains. (134)

If television was coming to enhance entertainment, natural gas was about to provide a new fuel for home and business. Early in 1947, the *Leader* announced that Limon seemed assured of natural gas once arrangements could be made for building a pipeline. Construction did not begin until the end of 1948. The job was finally completed in June 1949. (135)

Because of the coming of natural gas, Limon needed to upgrade and expand many municipal facilities. The fire department was one. Given that its equipment was old and rundown, the trustees appointed Chuck Stone the new fire chief and directed him to modernize the entire operation. One result came in 1949 when Limon replaced its pre-war Model A fire truck with a modern vehicle. At the same time the trustees supported plans for a permanent library building and a librarian — plans pushed largely by the women in town. These goals also became a reality in the course of the late 1940s and early 1950s largely through work spearheaded by Edith May Bell, Mrs. Clinton (Dorothy) Bell, and Mabel Haberthier. (136)

Other changes came, too. For the first time, the town put uniform street numbers on homes and businesses. A $100,000 gymnasium was added onto the high school. The trustees provided for garbage collection to address that very old problem. The town supported a flood control project to control further potential high waters in the Big Sandy (even if it was largely dry). There was interest in building a Limon Community Hospital (although in the end it was built in Hugo). There was constant discussion to get the State Highway Department to "oil" Highway 71, the main road south from Brush through Limon to Ordway. This project finally began in the early 1950s and enhanced Limon's role as the hub city of the high plains. (137)

Water shortages never seemed to go away, however, and that became a top priority for the trustees once the war ended. In 1945, under the leadership of

Mayor Ted Spaid, the council began to seek sources of more water. By mid-1946, the water committee had concluded that "the most desirable location for new wells" was on land in South Limon owned by the Safranek family. Frank Safranek had once been town attorney.

The problem facing the trustees was that the Safraneks did not wish to sell, or did not wish to sell at the price the town offered. On August 16, 1946, Mayor Spaid and the trustees met in special session. They resolved that it was "necessary for the health and safety" of the town to obtain additional water and that it had been "impossible" to reach an agreement with the Safraneks. As a result, they resolved to file a suit to condemn the land. Even though the town took possession, the Safraneks carried their fight against condemnation all the way to the United States Supreme Court, a suit that lasted nearly 50 years. Ultimately, in the early 1990s, the legal system upheld the town's actions. (138)

The trustees also envisioned an airport. The voters approved appropriations in 1946, and the trustees allowed the First National Bank of Limon to purchase the $10,000 in bonds at 2-1/4 percent interest. The town pledged its fullest cooperation with the federal government in building the facility. Yet the euphoria involved in developing an airport (a symbol of place and prosperity in 20th century America) was shortlived because funds were insufficient. Later, in 1951, came somber news from Flagler, just 30 miles away. Twenty people died in a stunt plane crash at the airport there. (139)

Another serious question pertained to public health. If the Spanish Influenza had carried off thousands in the wake of World War I, then polio spread the

The Limon Rail Yards 1941. Note the flooded Big Sandy south of town.

Limon Town Hall Collection

same fear in the wake of World War II. In July 1946, the board gave Dr. J.O. Clanin, Limon's public health officer, "full authority to act in any way he saw fit" to combat this scourge that attacked the nervous system, particularly of the young, and caused partial or full paralysis. The fear of contagion grew as football season approached. Some thought the practice season should be scratched. But in September, the trustees decided to allow practice to begin provided that all players dressed and changed uniforms at home. The gym was to be locked at all times, however, and young children kept away from practice.

Such concerns over polio persisted for several more years. Not until the mid-1950s did Jonas Salk develop a polio vaccine that ended the threat of polio. It then became common practice to receive the vaccine. (140)

Postwar developments in Limon also reflected two new, unprecedented features in American life — big government and the Cold War. In 1950, the trustees received a letter from the Federal Bureau of Investigation requesting the town's cooperation in Operation Road Block, designed to apprehend parties wanted by the agency. The town decided to cooperate. And in June 1950, with the Cold War in place, the trustees held a special meeting "for the purpose of setting up a local organization of civil defense." Former mayor A.C. Sinclair became the town's first civil defense director, and the town established various committees — mutual aid, evacuation, defense measures, health measures, and a military and integration committee. (141)

Perhaps a culminating point celebrating Limon's development came in 1952 when President Harry S. Truman stopped in Limon to give a speech. (142)

The famous crossing of the Rock Island and Union Pacific railroads, as it looked in 1941. The depot is in center; the Union Pacific track runs from top to bottom.

Limon Town Hall Collection

Limon's venerable Bank Hotel was the second home of the First National Bank of Limon, which, later in the 1990s, was to celebrate its 75th anniversary.

CONCLUSION

By the mid-20th century, Limon had emerged as the leading town in Lincoln County, but its growth and prosperity still reflected the factors which had brought it into being some seventy years before — its role as a transportation and distribution center. Technological change had altered that to some degree, but in the 1950s, Limon still served the farms and ranches of the high plains. It was the place where wheat and cattle and other products could be shipped to market and where agricultural needs could be met. Limon also served more rural areas as a social and educational center.

From the 1880s to the 1950s, the Rock Island and the Union Pacific railroads, which had brought Limon into being, continued to be important as a source of jobs and a haven for travelers. But the railroads' role gradually declined as the role of cars, trucks, and highways grew. Cars and trucks not only created new jobs for garages, gas stations, motels, and restaurants, but also had another impact — they reoriented Limon physically from a town organized to support the railroads to one in which the railroads remained important, but one increasingly focused on trucks and automobiles, truckers, and tourists. With American railroads in general and passenger traffic in particular going into decline after World War II, Limon fell into part of this process and the town's reorientation reflected it. Those changes would be even greater as Limon moved into the second half of the 20th century.

Postscript

In 1952, the individuals, families, and companies that were to move Limon forward were beginning to emerge. Later in the 1990s, a gift of a Rock Island baggage wagon from the pioneer Homer Monks family and a caboose from the Union Pacific Railroad led to the development of the Limon Heritage Society and continuing efforts to involve townspeople as stewards in preserving the community's past through support of Colorado Preservation 2000.

The Limon Heritage Museum as it appeared in the 1990s.

In the mid-1990s, a Prairie Monument, located next to an 1892 cattle scale in the Museum's Railroad Park, honored all eastern plains pioneer families.

Dedication of an Eclipse windmill at June 1996 Western Festival ceremonies in the Railroad park, paid tribute to early settlers of the high plains.

FOOTNOTES

(1) Doty and McFarland, "Rocketing to the Rockies, " 60.
(2) Marvis June Marshall, "Jottings About Town," *The Limon Leader,* January 1950.
(3) Whittemore, *Illustrated History of Ranching,* 33-34.
(4) Hugo *Range Ledger,* March 27, 1902; Whittemore, *Illustrated History of Ranching,* 11-13.
(5) *Colorado State Business Directory,* (Denver: Ives Publishing Company, 1893), 548-59.
(6) *Colorado State Business Directories,* 1893-1900.
(7) *The Limon Leader,* March 10, 1944.
(8) Glen Raymond Coonts Interview, 1977, Limon Public Library, Limon, Colorado. [LPL]
(9) Nate and Ida Einertson, Mrs. Drier and Mrs. Esther Johnson Interviews, LPL.
(10) Drier and Johnson Interviews, LPL.
(11) Drier Interview, LPL.
(12) Drier Interview, LPL.
(13) Coonts, Drier, and Johnson Interviews, LPL.
(14) Einertson, Johnson Interviews, LPL.
(15) Einertson, Johnson Interviews, LPL.
(16) Einertson, Martha Kollath Interviews, LPL; *The Limon Leader,* March 10, 1944.
(17) Stewart and Stewart, *Colorado Newspapers, Editors, Owners,* 322-23.
(18) "My Home Town" plus Mrs. Elmo DeGarmo Rasmus to *The Limon Leader,* Mt. Pleasant, Iowa, August 27, 1967, LPL.
(19) Mrs. Elmo DeGarmo Rasmus to *The Limon Leader,* LPL.
(20) Mrs. Elmo DeGarmo Rasmus to *The Limon Leader,* LPL.
(21) *The Limon Leader,* September 25, 1975. "Sixtieth Anniversary, The First Methodist Church, Limon, Colorado," October 16, 1960, LPL.
(22) "History of the Baptist Church, Limon, Colorado," LPL.
(23) "My Home Town," August 27, 1967, LPL.
(24) *The Limon Leader,* September 25, 1975, LPL.
(25) *Colorado State Business Directory,* (1895-1910), *passim.*
(26) Obituary, *The Limon Leader,* July 10, 1942.
(27) *Eastern Colorado Plainsman* & the *Range Ledger,* July 10, 1942.
(28) W. S. Pershing To Whom It May Concern, Limon, Colorado, September 20, 1909, Limon Town Board Minutes. [LTBM]
(29) T.J. Newkirk to W.S. Pershing, Chicago, Illinois, September 10, 1909, and W. S. Pershing To Whom It May Concern, Limon, Colorado, September 20, 1909, LTBM.
(30) Document 133; copy of poll book of election in re: Incorporation of Town of Limon, County Court, Lincoln County, filed October 26, 1909, LTBM.
(31) 1910 and 1911, LTBM.
(32) 1910 and 1911, LTBM.
(33) June 10, July 15, 1915, LTBM.
(34) May 4, 1916, LTBM.
(35) February 1, 1917; January 4, 1917, LTBM.
(36) July 3, August 11, 1919, LTBM.
(37) August 2, September 6, November 1, December 6, 15, 1917, LTBM.
(38) January, March 6, 1919, LTBM.
(39) September 4, 1919, LTBM.
(40) George H. Sethman to Carl M. Cook, Denver, February 15, March 12, 1915, December 3, 1915; Resolution, March 4, 1915, LTBM.
(41) Resolution, April 23, 1915; Notice to Constructors, and Local Improvement Bond; April 29, May 12, 13, LTBM.

(42) Sethman to Cook, Denver, December 7, 1915, December 3, 1915, LTBM.
(43) February 21, July 6, 1916, LTBM.
(44) Limon *Herald*, May 23, 1918, LPL.
(45) Limon *Herald*, October 17, 1918, LPL.
(46) Charles W. Stone Questionnaire, Limon Heritage Society. [LHS]
(47) Limon *Herald*, October 17, 1918, LPL.
(48) February 7, April 2 and 16, 1914, LTBM.
(49) October 7, 1920, LTBM.
(50) January 3, 1924, and *passim*, LTBM.
(51) May 1, July 1, 1920, LTBM.
(52) October 22, 1920; Ordinance #45, LTBM.
(53) April 15, 1915; For more see May 1, 1917, LTBM.
(54) April 5, 1917, LTBM.
(55) July 4, 1929, LTBM.
(56) February 7, 1918, LTBM.
(57) April 17, 1919, LTBM.
(58) Various minutes, April 28 through September, 1920, LTBM.
(59) November 4, 1920, LTBM.
(60) December 2, 1920, LTBM.
(61) Stone Questionnaire, LHS.
(62) Stone Questionnaire, LHS.
(63) Stone Questionnaire, LHS.
(64) June 1, 1922, June 4, 1925, LTBM.
(65) January 3, 1923, LTBM.
(66) June, 1, 1922; March 6, July 3, October 2, 1924; March 14, June 4, 1925, LTBM.
(67) October 17, November 5, 1925, LTBM.
(68) January 21, May 6, 1926; January 6, March 3, 1927, LTBM.
(69) March 3, April 7, 1927, LTBM. The sale price was apparently $45,000; See June 7, 1928, LTBM.
(70) October 6, November 3, 1927, LTBM.
(71) March 1, 1923, LTBM.
(72) May 3, May 16, June 7, 1923, LTBM.
(73) May 3, 1923, LTBM.
(74) November 7, 1929, LTBM. (E Street was known as Booster Avenue in early Limon.)
(75) Reprinted in *The Regional Review*, Vol. 13, No. 2, June 1990, LPL.
(76) August 7, 1930, LTBM.
(77) June 2, 1927; May 3, June 7, 1928, LTBM.
(78) March 2, June 7, 1928, LTBM.
(79) June 7, 1928, LTBM.
(80) Doty and McFarland, 60-61; June 2, 1932, LTBM.
(81) July 1, 1930, LTBM. *Passim.*, Winter, 1930-31, LTBM.
(82) July 8, August 6, 1931; February 4, 1932, LTBM.
(83) February 5, 1931, LTBM.
(84) May 7, June 4, July 8, August 6, 1931, LTBM.
(85) December 3, 1931, LTBM.
(86) January 7, 1932, LTBM.
(87) March 3, 19, 1932, LTBM.
(88) January 7, 1932, LTBM.
(89) John J. (Jack) and Norma Grenawalt Questionnaire, LHS.
(90) Stone Questionnaire, LHS.
(91) Grenawalt Questionnaire, LHS.

(92) Doris Akers Questionnaire, LHS.
(93) April 7, 1932, LTBM.
(94) April 14, 1932, LTBM.
(95) November 3, 1932, LTBM.
(96) April 14, 1932, LTBM.
(97) September 1, 1932, LTBM.
(98) See first, November 6, 1931; May 5, November 3, 1932, LTBM.
(99) November 3, 1932, LTBM.
(100) November 3, December 1, 1932; January 5, 1933, LTBM.
(101) January 5, 1933, LTBM.
(102) February 5, 16, 1931; June 2, September 1, 1932, LTBM.
(103) December 4, 1930; June 4, 1931, LTBM.
(104) Margaret M. Vermillion Questionnaire, LHS.
(105) Stone, Grenawalt Questionnaires, LHS.
(106) Grenawalt, Helen Christenson, Akers, Cleo and Luella Steele Interviews, LHS.
(107) Irma Kjosness Questionnaire, LHS.
(108) June 4, July 8, 1931, LTBM.
(109) *The Limon Leader*, June 2, 1944.
(110) Kjosness, Stone, Grenawalt, Minnie Coonts, Gladys Lusk, Gloria Campbell Lee Questionnaires, LHS.
(111) Lee, Kjosness Questionnaires, and others, LHS.
(112) Doty and McFarland, 61.
(113) *The Limon Leader*, January 4, February 18, March 3, 1944; April 1, 1943, LTBM.
(114) Lee, Kjosness, Steele Questionnaires, LHS.
(115) *The Limon Leader*, August 28, 1944; Kjosness Questionnaire, LHS.
(116) Grenawalt Questionnaire, LHS; April 1, 1943, LTBM.
(117) Vermillion Interview, LHS.
(118) Stone, Grenawalt Interviews, LHS.
(119) *The Limon Leader*, March 10, May 19, 1944.
(120) Lusk Questionnaire, LHS; *The Limon Leader*, May 19, 1944; February 12, 1943.
(121) *The Limon Leader*, February 12, April 23, May 28, October 1, 1943; February 18, 25, March 10, 1944.
(122) *The Limon Leader*, October 1, 1943; February 18, 1944; February 25, March 10, 1944.
(123) *The Limon Leader*, March 17, April 7, 1944.
(124) *The Limon Leader*, January 14, 21, 1944.
(125) *The Limon Leader*, January 14, 1944.
(126) *The Limon Leader*, February 5, March 3, 1944.
(127) *The Limon Leader*, April 9, August 20, October 1, 1943; March 10, 1944; April 28, May 26, June 9, July 28, 1944; November 17, December 1, 1944.
(128) July 1, August 5, 1943, LTBM.
(129) March 2, November 2, 1944, LTBM.
(130) February 3, April 6, 1944, LTBM; *The Limon Leader*, February 25, 1944.
(131) *The Limon Leader*, April 25, 1947; June 4, July 23, 1948; April 22, July 18, 1949; August 18, November 14, 1952.
(132) Doty and McFarland, 61.
(133) *The Limon Leader*, February 14, 1947; April 25, 1951.
(134) *The Limon Leader*, April 1, August 22, December 5, 1947; June 24, 1949; May 2, 1952.
(135) *The Limon Leader*, February 14, May 16, 1947; October 1, 1948; June 3, 1949.
(136) *The Limon Leader*, January 21, June 17, 1949; April 20, 1951.

(137) *The Limon Leader*, January 28, February 4, July 29, September 22, 1949; November 24, 1950, May 25, 1951; January 9, 1953.
(138) August 16, 1946, LTBM.
(139) June 6, September 13, 1946, LTBM; *The Limon Leader*, September 21, 1951.
(140) July 11, September 13, 1946, LTBM.
(141) May 4, June 4, 1950, LTBM.
(142) *The Limon Leader*, September 26, October 10, 1952.

BIBLIOGRAPHY

Primary Sources

Interviews, Limon Public Library.

Minutes, Limon Board of Trustees, 1909-1953, Limon, Colorado.

Questionnaires, Limon Heritage Society.

Books

Cooley, Dale, and Mary Liz Owen, *Where the Wagons Rolled: The History of Lincoln County and the People Who Came Before 1925*. Limon, Colorado: Eastern Colorado Printery, 1985.

Whittemore, Loren R., *An Illustrated History of Ranching in the Pikes Peak Region*. Colorado Springs: Denton-Berkland Print Co., 1967.

Newspapers

Eastern Colorado Plainsman and the *Range Ledger.*

Hugo *Range Ledger*

Limon *Herald*

The Limon Leader

Other publications

Colorado State Business Directories (1890-1947)

Articles

Doty, Michael C., and E.M. "Mel" McFarland, "Rocketing to the Rockies," *Colorado Rail Annual*, No. 17, Golden: Colorado Railroad Museum, 1987.

UNITED—in Soul Searching Ideals

YOU'RE confused by the cross currents of world affairs, by uncertainty about the future? Sure you are, Mr. Smith. You are going through an experience unlike anything you have known before. And it makes you none too happy. But, frankly, that unhappiness is not without a comforting thought. For years a good many of us, millions of our fellow Americans, had become too indifferent for our real good—and ideals, yes, American ideals were something only vaguely connected with our lives.

Yet now when you find yourself alone and thinking about this world of bleeding hearts, you somehow wish there was something hard and firm a man could cling to—something that wouldn't melt away like riches and false pride, or like that dish of ice cream you had for dessert tonight.

You need something, Mr. Smith. You haven't realized it before, perhaps, because you've had pretty fair security. Never rich, of course, but compared to those poor devils in Poland and France and Greece you were a king. That was before you saw America threatened, before they made a soldier out of Junior and began to get excited about this national defense business. It's a fine thing to be an American, Mr. Smith, but doggone it, there are too many people in your frame of mind nowadays—people who are groping for something to get their hands on—something hard and firm!

Those Pilgrims had it back in 1620. Remember? It took something to sail a rickety little ship across the Atlantic when you knew that your only reception would come from hostile Indians, when you knew that hunger and maybe even death lay in the cards.

Those barefooted, frozen, starving wretches had it at Valley Forge, too, something they could cling to. That "Something" is kind of an American heritage, we guess. It gave Lincoln courage, and it tramped across the western prairies beside pioneer wagon trains.

Know what it is, Mr. Smith?

We call it—Faith.

You see, Faith is what gives strength, without which all the airplanes and soldiers and machine guns in the world are useless. Faith is what makes you get up when they knock you down. Faith in the eternal values. Faith in Divine justice and in the blessings of a UNITED States of America, a nation indivisible, dedicated to life, liberty, and the pursuit of happiness. Faith in soul searching ideals.

You can get your hands on Faith. Won't you try it?

These patriotic thoughts are presented by the cooperation of the following citizens .

The First National Bank of Limon
M. E. HARRIS — Cleaner - Clothier
Limon Motor Co. — Ford Sales and Service
Spaid Motor Co. — Expert Motor Repairing
HOUTZ DRUG CO. — Phone 83
GAMBLE STORE Authorized Dealer — Used Tires and Tubes
Harold Lee Sinclair Service — Washing and Greasing
Jaggers' Hdw. & Furn. Co.
Limon Body Shop — Metal Work and Painting
Harris Motor Co. — Used Tires and Parts
The Trinidad Bean & Elev. Co.
Farmers Grain and Bean Assn. — Grain — Beans — Feed — Storage
Mariner's Service Station — Tire Repairs and Battery Work
Commonwealth Utilities Corp.

Grease Spot Super Station — Real Service at no Extra Cost
The Quist-Holmes Co. — "Where Equipment and Parts are Available"
The Arapahoe Food Store — "Pay Cash and Save the Difference"
H. V. KELLER — Jeweler - Optometrist
Martin's Shoe Shop — Invisible Half Soling
The Style Shop — Nelly Don Dresses - Betty Rose Coats and Suits
Betty's Liquor Store
Myrtle's Beauty Shop — Expert Hair Styling
CANTWELL'S — Hardware — Variety Merchandise
Landis Cafe
The Merchants Cafe — "Always the Best"
Sinclair Refining Co. — Chas. E. Kennedy, Agent
Seal Funeral Home

Hord Mercantile Co.
Continental Oil Company — Lloyd Kimble, Agent
BILLIE'S CAFE — Open All Night
WARNICK'S — Clothing - Hats - Shoes
Dougherty Radio Shop — Radio Batteries, Tubes and Repairs
Highway Liquor Store — "A Good Place to Trade"
Cope Service Station — Conoco Products
Foster Lumber Company
Cozy Cafe and Bar — "A Good Place to Stop on the Highway"
Gray Motor Co. — Chrysler - Plymouth
The Eastern Colorado Leader
Earl's Piggly Wiggly — John Freel, Mgr.
Auto Service Company — "Complete Automotive Service"
Cactus Theatre

Limon businesses joined to support the World War II effort as its outcome appeared uncertain in May 1942. Fifty years later, in the 1990s, one business remained with the same name—The First National Bank of Limon. However, Commonwealth Utilities Corp. (later Mountain View Electric Association, Inc.), the Eastern Colorado Leader (later The Limon Leader), Auto Service Company (later Auto Service and Supply Co., Inc.), Houtz Drug (later Hoffman Drug), and Sinclair Refining Co. (later D-J Petroleum Inc.) continued serving the high plains. *The Eastern Colorado Leader and The Genoa Sentinel, May 22, 1942.*